David Self has been a freelanc[...] years, specializing in literary, [...] has published books on the problem of suffering, the lives of the saints and on the world faiths; he also writes a weekly column for school assembly leaders in the *Times Educational Supplement*. He is a winner of the Sandford St Martin Prize for religious broadcasting and a communicant member of the Church of England. He lives in the Cambridgeshire Fens.

for Eric

# The Roots of Christian Festivals

David Self

First published in Great Britain in 2004 by
SPCK
Holy Trinity
Marylebone Road
London NW1 4DU

SPCK does not necessarily endorse the individual views
contained in its publications.

British Library Cataloguing-in-Publication Data

A catalogue record for this book is available from the British Library

ISBN 0–281–05681–1

1 3 5 7 9 10 8 6 4 2

Typeset by Avocet Typeset, Chilton, Aylesbury, Bucks
Printed in Great Britain by Bookmarque Ltd, Croydon, Surrey

# *Contents*

# Contents

# *Introduction*

It is natural to measure out our lives by our own personal landmarks. 'That was the year John was born.' 'Next week, it'll be my birthday. That means it's only a month to Christmas. Then we can plan next year's holiday.' Our year is enlivened by our domestic anniversaries and rituals – and by those celebrated by society at large. One has only to keep an eye on shops selling greetings cards to gain evidence of these punctuation marks in our calendar: St Valentine's Day, Mother's Day and so on.

The pre-Christian, pagan world understood this need to sprinkle the year with festivals and their associated rituals very well. Primarily, that society divided its year into quarters or seasons. The spring (or vernal) and the autumn equinoxes when the day is of equal length with the night were both major festivals. Of these, Beltane was the spring celebration, elements of which survive in folkloric May Day customs; Samhain was the autumn one out of which has grown Hallowe'en. Midsummer Day and a winter festival of light were the other two turning points.

For the first Christians, the one great festival was Sunday. Every seven days, the first day of the week was a major celebration of the resurrection of Jesus Christ. As the years and centuries passed, the Church came to make a special, annual observance of that event and so developed the season of Easter. Christmas and other festivals and fasts became established later – the theological roots of these being, of course, the events in the life of Christ (and the coming of the Holy Spirit) that they commemorated.

But as Christianity spread throughout the Roman Empire, its missionaries not only had to teach its truths but to woo their converts away from traditional observances and celebrations – many of which were obviously very enjoyable. It was natural, therefore, that some Christian festivals should have been grafted onto the flourishing pagan ones. So the pre-Christian winter festival of light was trimmed and nurtured to become Christmas, the mid-February 'Feast of Lights' became Candlemas and Samhain evolved into All Saints. By the late Middle Ages, when a considerable number of saints' days were also holy days (and holidays), a farm labourer had a great many days off work each year – certainly enough to make today's workers extremely envious.

Then came the Reformation. The number of saints' days was cut back to the Gospel saints (as is clear from the Book of Common Prayer). The ascent of Puritanism and the Commonwealth further abolished many celebrations (even Christmas) and, while many were reinstated following the Restoration, others were forgotten. What more effectively pruned the calendar of many of its festivals was the Industrial Revolution. The urbanization of the workforce and factory owners eager to make every possible gain from their new machines resulted in the abolition of all but a very few holidays. Rogation and Lammas had little place in urban life. But with increased leisure in subsequent decades, some observances were revived. Then came the rapid secularization of society in the second half of the twentieth century which resulted in many religious festivals surviving only in the liturgical calendar. Advent, Ascensiontide and Pentecost make little impact on society at large.

What is interesting is that, in this empty field, a number of secular festivals have sprouted – to fill our hunger for markers through the year. Television provides some annual events:

Children in Need and Red Nose Day among others. The sporting world provides many more: Grand National Day, the Cup Final and Wimbledon mark out the spring and early summer. The commercial world creates its own festivals: Father's Day, for one. And festivals once Christianized but later neglected have, like untended plants, run wild – notably Hallowe'en.

This book aims first to unearth the roots and then to describe the growth (or decline) of the principal markers of the Christian year. Also included are some modern 'inventions' such as Christian Aid Week, Remembrance Sunday and Thanksgiving which (while not reflecting biblical events) figure prominently in many churches' calendars. Second, it sets out to describe some of the ecclesiastical and social customs that have accrued to these festivals.

While the observance of festivals varies greatly from one Christian tradition to another, it is hoped that this introduction to the subject will help readers of whatever tradition (or indeed of none) to understand an important part of our common heritage and ways of celebrating the faith.

# *Advent*

*Advent is the ecclesiastical season immediately before Christmas and is observed as a time of penitence and preparation not only for Christmas but also for the Second Coming of Christ. The first Sunday of Advent marks the beginning of the Church's year.*

In the secular world, the period before Christmas is now seen as part of that festival. It has become a time of frenzied preparation devoted to Christmas shopping, office parties, and the buying and sending of Christmas cards. Shops and many homes are decorated well before Christmas and in town centres the Christmas lights may be lit as early as November.

For Christians, this season of the year is a time of preparation of rather a different nature. Its name, Advent, comes from the Latin *adventius*, meaning coming or arrival, and so Advent is often said to be a time of waiting for the arrival of Christmas, the coming of Jesus to earth as a baby in Bethlehem. Many of the Advent hymns take up this theme – such as 'O come, O come Emmanuel' ('Emmanuel' being an old word meaning 'God is with us'). This means Advent is a penitential season: a time for self-assessment and for confession of failures. It is a time when people resolve to do better in the future; 'to put things right for when Jesus comes' or, as it was once more formally expressed, 'to prepare themselves worthily to celebrate the anniversary of the Lord's coming into the world'.

But Advent is not simply a period of preparation for the Incarnation. It looks forward to the Second Coming of Christ – as described in St Matthew's Gospel, chapter 24. For this reason, it became customary for sermons during Advent to focus on 'the Four Last Things', these being heaven, hell, death and judgement.

Because it was conceived as a penitential season, Advent originated as a fast of forty days (like Lent), beginning on the day after St Martin's Day, which falls on 11 November. For this reason, it was known as early as the fifth century as 'St Martin's Lent'. In fact, the origin of Advent cannot have been much earlier than this because there is no evidence of Christmas being observed on 25 December before the end of the fourth century. Advent was reduced to its present length in the ninth century.

Since then, it has begun on the Sunday nearest to St Andrew's Day (30 November) and includes four Sundays. This means that the earliest it can begin is 27 November, in which case Advent lasts twenty-eight days. Its latest possible starting date is 3 December, when Advent will have only twenty-one days. If the fourth Sunday of Advent should fall on 24 December, then the Church traditionally ruled that the Advent fast lasted until sunset on that day – at which time it became Christmas Eve. In the modern high street and shopping mall, this moment now seems to indicate the end not of Advent but of Christmas: down come the decorations and up go advertisements for the post-Christmas sales!

Because of its penitential nature, weddings were not celebrated during this season. Many churches still do not have flowers on their altars during Advent, while priests and ministers wear purple vestments, symbolizing humility and penitence. The joyful hymn of praise known as the *Te Deum* is omitted from Morning Prayer and the *Gloria in Excelsis* is not said or sung during Holy Communion services. Some brave clergy still try to delay the singing of Christmas carols until Christmas Eve.

While there may be no flowers in churches during Advent, it is likely there will be an Advent wreath. It has its origins in pre-Christian Germany when people made wreaths of evergreen and lit fires as signs of hope for the coming spring and longer hours of daylight. Christians preserved the custom and by the sixteenth century Advent wreaths were to be found in both Catholic and Lutheran homes. It was only in the middle of the twentieth century that they became a common feature in churches.

Traditionally, four candles (one for each Sunday) are set in the ring with a fifth, larger candle at its centre. Three of the four outer candles are purple (the liturgical colour for Advent), while the other one is pink or rose-coloured. On Advent Sunday, one purple candle is lit, as a prayer is said. On the second Sunday, two purple ones are lit. Then, on the third Sunday, the pink candle is lit, as well as the first two purple ones. The reason for this Sunday's candle being pink stems from the fact that the Roman Catholic mass for this day is more cheerful in tone than on the other Advent Sundays, asking congregations to rejoice that 'the Lord is now nigh and close at hand'. On this day, the mass used to begin with the Latin words *Gaudete in Domino* (Rejoice in the Lord). As a result, it became known as Gaudete Sunday and remains a day when some Catholic churches use pink rather than purple vestments and flowers are permitted on altars to reflect the mood of joy. It is an odd fact that Lutheran families maintained this tradition in their homes when choosing candles for their Advent wreaths.

The final purple candle is lit on the fourth Sunday, while the white candle (representing Christ, the light of the world) is lit on Christmas Day. This sequence emphasizes the message of the Advent wreath: as Christmas, with the coming of Jesus, gets nearer and nearer, the greater is the light burning in the darkness of winter. Out of darkness comes light.

Other Advent customs include counting its days by making chalk marks on a door frame and the making or buying of Advent calendars. These became popular in the middle of the nineteenth century as a way of helping children to count the days to Christmas. Usually they have twenty-four 'windows', perhaps because the secular world imagines Advent as starting on 1 December. Each window opens up to show a picture linked with this time of year. One may show an angel or one of the shepherds who visited the baby Jesus. Others may show pictures of Christmas presents, and the last window to be opened usually shows Jesus himself, lying in the manger. Commercial calendars often have windows that open to reveal chocolates or sweets – an idea far removed from the concept of Advent as a fast. The first calendar containing a chocolate for each day was made in 1958.

As we have already said, the Christian year follows the life of Jesus, starting with Advent. Advent Sunday can consequently be said to be the Church's New Year's Day.

# St Nicholas and St Lucia

*Pre-Christmas customs associated with St Nicholas are said to have given rise to the comparatively modern legend of Santa Claus or Father Christmas, while St Lucia, little known in English-speaking countries, figures prominently in Swedish tradition. Their saints' days are, respectively, 6 December and 13 December.*

All Dutch children know that St Nicholas (or Sinterklaas as they nickname him – his name in Dutch is actually *Sint Niklaasje*) lives in Spain. And they know that, each year, in the early days of December he and his friend, commonly called Black Peter, visit the Netherlands, which is why they sing:

> Look, there is the steamer from faraway lands,
> It brings us St Nicholas; he's waving his hands,
> His horse is a-prancing on deck, up and down,
> The banners are waving in village and town.

This tradition is acted out each December in Amsterdam and in other places in the Netherlands. St Nicholas arrives, wearing a bishop's cope and mitre. He has a white beard, white gloves and a white horse. Seated on his horse, he rides round the city with Peter walking at his side. People cheer him, church bells ring and there is often a band leading his procession with policemen on motorbikes as outriders. And later on, so young Dutch children believe, St Nicholas and Peter will visit every child who has been well behaved during the last year in order to leave him or her a present.

The real St Nicholas lived in the fourth century, not in Spain but in Myra on the southern coast of what is now Turkey. Nicholas was Bishop of Myra and was (it is said) rich, generous and shy. Consequently, he chose to do good by stealth. One well-known story tells how Bishop Nicholas accidentally overheard three young women grumbling about being poor – so poor that nobody would marry them. Nicholas then heard their father join them and say how sorry he was that he had no job and little hope of earning any money to pay for their weddings. That night, Nicholas returned to their house and threw a large bag of gold coins in through an open window.

Next morning, the father and his daughters awoke to find the bag of gold. 'Well,' said the father, 'now my eldest daughter can get married.' And, so the story goes, a handsome young man fell in love with her, the father paid for a splendid wedding and all was well. Except that the other two daughters were still unhappy. Nicholas again chanced to overhear their grumbles. That night, as before, he threw a bag of gold in through their open window. And again, as before, the following morning they found the gold. Soon the second daughter was married. Some days later, Nicholas heard the father and youngest daughter quietly lamenting there was no money for a third wedding. Later, Nicholas returned to leave a third bag of gold, but this time the father heard him and came to the door. Nicholas tried to escape, but the father caught him by the arm and tried to thank him. Nicholas said that he should rather give thanks to God who had given Nicholas money to use well. It is this story or legend that led people to believe St Nicholas goes round giving presents to those who deserve them.

When Dutch people emigrated from the Netherlands to the

United States of America, they settled in what was originally called New Amsterdam but is now New York. There they maintained the custom and St Nicholas (in his red bishop's robes and with his white beard) went round the city, distributing presents. When other New Yorkers heard the Dutch immigrants calling him Sinterklaas, they thought they were saying 'Santa Claus'. An American poet, Clement Clarke Moore, embroidered the event in a poem, beginning:

> 'Twas the night before Christmas, when all through
> the house
> Not a creature was stirring, not even a mouse;
> The stockings were hung by the chimney with care
> In hopes that St Nicholas soon would be there.

From this developed the legend of Santa Claus, a tradition which was then exported back to other European countries, giving rise to the modern Father Christmas. It has subsequently spread further afield where it has been further modified. In Kenya for example, where Christmas is warm and sunny, Father Christmas travels by donkey.

In Sweden, it is not St Nicholas but St Lucia who figures prominently in the pre-Christmas festivities. Either the oldest or youngest daughter of a family gets up early and, wearing a white dress with a red sash, takes a tray of coffee and cakes called *Lussekatts*, which are baked the day before, upstairs to the rest of the family. On her head, she wears a crown of evergreen leaves in which are set five white candles. Nowadays, battery-operated electric lights commonly replace the candles for safety reasons. Schools, offices and towns sometimes choose or elect their own Lucias.

Many believe this is done in memory of St Lucia, who was an Italian, possibly Sicilian, Christian girl living in the second century. Because Christians within the Roman Empire were then persecuted, they met to pray in secret. Lucia, it is said, carried trays of food at night to their secret meeting places. So that her hands were free to carry the food, she wore lights on her head to help her see where she was going.

It is a matter of debate whether Swedish Lucia customs reflect this story. Others say that these customs were brought to Sweden in the seventeenth century by Protestant Germans who had settled there. For them, the girl chosen to be Lucia represented the Christ Child, who delivered Christmas gifts, rather than Nicholas who was perceived to be Catholic.

# Christmas Eve

*Historically, the night before Christmas has never been a festival in its own right but simply the eve of the Christmas feast. Over the years, however, it has acquired a number of distinctive customs and the Church of England in its modern service book* Common Worship *now terms it a lesser festival.*

Traditionally, Christmas Eve is the time for decorating the home. These days the decorations are likely to be tinsel, the holly plastic and the tree fibre-optic. It wasn't always so. An anonymous Victorian described a nineteenth-century Christmas Eve in this way:

> On Christmas Eve a great quantity of holly and of laurel is brought in from the garden and from the farm. This greenery is put up all over the house in every room just before it becomes dark on that day. Then there is brought into the hall a young pine tree, about twice the height of a man, to service for a Christmas tree, and on this innumerable little candles are fixed, and presents for all the household and the guests and the children of the village.

The custom of bringing a fir tree indoors and decorating it for Christmas originated in Germany, and it was Prince Albert, the German husband of Queen Victoria, who popularized it in Britain. Holly, ivy and mistletoe were, however, used as winter decorations long before 'Christmas' trees became commonplace. Because they are evergreens, they have long been seen as symbols of eternal life. Mistletoe in particular was regarded as a sacred plant by, for example, the Druids in the pre-Christian era. It was used as a cure for everything from epilepsy to toothache while holly was said to be a protection against fire and storms.

Another tradition associated with Christmas Eve is the custom of 'bringing home the yule log', Yule being the name of a pagan festival celebrated at the winter solstice in northern Europe before the coming of Christianity. Custom dictated that the log had to be very large, from an oak tree and too heavy for one man to lift – so the master of the house and his servant brought it indoors together and cast it on the fire in the open hearth of the farmstead or house. Superstition said that if it burned all night and was found still smouldering in the morning, the home would be prosperous for the coming year.

Fire and candles were important to primitive peoples in the northern hemisphere. As the days got shorter, they were a reminder that light would soon return to the world. Indeed, some people thought that by burning yule logs, they would give new strength to the dying sun. As Christianity began to spread northwards through Europe, it borrowed and adapted many of these customs as a way of showing how Jesus brought light into a dark world. As the centuries went by, it added its own observances.

In the year 1223, the man we now know as St Francis created what has become a popular Christmas tradition often associated with Christmas Eve: the crib or nativity scene. That year, some of those who had joined Francis as 'brothers' or friars (and were following the rule or way of life he had laid down) were living in an Italian village called Greccio, high up a river valley near the ancient city of Rieti. Tradition has it that Francis asked a fellow friar,

Brother John, to help him make a tableau of the scene in the Bethlehem stable to help teach the people of Greccio the mystery of the Incarnation. John made all the necessary arrangements in a hillside cave, placing a manger full of hay in the cave and having an ox and an ass standing by.

On Christmas Eve, Francis asked the people of the district each to bring a lighted candle and come with him to the cave. This they did, climbing up the mountain path. At the entrance to the cave was the manger, and around it were people dressed up to represent Mary, Joseph and the shepherds. In front of that manger, the first Christmas crib, a priest conducted a Holy Communion service. Today there is a convent at Greccio where followers of St Francis still live. Each Christmas Eve, the nativity is remembered not only there but all around the world as Christians act out that scene at Christmas as a nativity play or create cribs using model or miniature figures.

More recent in origin is the Christingle service. These were devised originally by Moravians (a Protestant Church in middle Europe) who wanted to create a distinctively Christian symbol. This resulted in the christingle. It consists of an orange (signifying God's world), surrounded by a red ribbon (to remind us of Christ's blood, shed for the world) and pierced by four sticks, which in practice are usually wooden cocktail sticks. On each of these are one or two nuts and raisins, symbolizing the fruits of the world. Inserted into the top of the orange is a small, lighted white candle, representing Jesus himself – the light of the world. At Christingle services, carols are sung and children often bring gifts for those less fortunate than themselves. In return, each child receives a christingle.

Another custom stemming from the Christmas Eve event at Greccio is the now widely held Christmas Eve Midnight Mass. The word 'mass', used by Catholic Christians, comes from a Latin word *missa* which occurs in the service. But for all Christians, both the Christmas crib and the midnight Communion service are reminders of the birth of the Christ Child some two thousand years ago – and the start of Christmas Day itself.

# *Christmas Day*

*For the majority of people in the western world, Christmas is the principal festival of the year and is now seen by many as a purely secular event. For the Christian, it remains a celebration of God's incarnation in the Christ Child and is widely regarded as second only to Easter in its importance.*

Irving Berlin's 'White Christmas' is one of the most popular secular Christmas songs of all time. It articulates the widespread association of snow with the Christmas feast that is part of popular culture throughout northern Europe and North America. But one thing we can say about the first Christmas Day when Jesus was born in Bethlehem is that it almost certainly wasn't snowing. Shepherds would not have kept their flocks out in such weather. Indeed, December is often a rainy time of the year in that part of the world. It is unlikely that sheep would have been out overnight on a hillside at that time, whatever the weather. It is also unlikely (but not impossible) that the Romans would have conducted a census, involving the movement of large parts of the population, during the winter months.

All of which suggests that the nativity probably did not occur in December. In fact, we do not know what time of the year it took place – unlike Easter which we know coincided with the Jewish spring festival of Passover. When Matthew and Luke came to write their Gospels, neither thought to specify the time of year. However, in the centuries following the birth of Jesus, Christians obviously wanted to observe a given day each year as a commemoration of the event.

The first evidence of such a festival comes from Egypt. About the year AD 200, 'certain Egyptian theologians' (according to the theologian Clement of Alexandria) placed Christ's birth on 20 May in the twenty-eighth year of the reign of Augustus. We also know that, by the end of the fourth century, Christians in Cyprus and Mesopotamia were celebrating the feast on 6 January, a custom still followed by many Orthodox Christians, especially in the Armenian Church. There also exists a reference in the writings of the fathers of the early Church to 'the Childhood Feast' being celebrated on that date in Jerusalem, with the bishop having travelled the six miles to Bethlehem for a service there the night before.

Various other historical references indicate considerable debate about the 'true' date. However, we know that the nativity was being celebrated in Rome on 25 December by the year 354; and that from the fourth century every western calendar assigns it to 25 December.

One reason the early Church may have had for selecting 25 December as Christmas Day was that it already was a holiday throughout the Roman Empire. In Latin, it was called *dies natalis invicti solis*, meaning 'the birthday of the unconquered sun'. It celebrated the fact that the shortest day of the winter was over, the days were now getting longer and the sun, instead of being 'conquered' by the winter cold, was getting stronger as another summer approached. The Church seized upon this custom to teach that Jesus was a new 'sun' or light coming into the world. As St John Chrysostom expressed it, 'Who is so unconquered as our Lord?'

Until the tenth century and the development of the season of Advent, the liturgical year was also considered as beginning on Christmas Day. A meeting of church leaders in the year 566 (or 567) known as the Second Council of Tours proclaimed the 'sanctity' of the Twelve Days of Christmas: that is, the twelve days were to be holy days – or holidays. The English word 'Christmas' is first found in Old English as 'Cristes Maesse' or the mass of Christ in the year 1038, and again as 'Cristes-messe' in 1131. The French name *Noël*, which is also widely used in English, is derived from the Latin *dies natalis*. By the time Cromwell and the Puritans had established the Commonwealth in England, the whole concept of Christmas was seen as 'popish', perhaps because of its Catholic-sounding name. Consequently, Christmas was forbidden throughout England by Act of Parliament in 1644. The day was to be observed as a fast but also a market day. Shops were compelled to open; plum puddings and mince pies were condemned as heathen. This Act was repealed with the Restoration of the monarchy in 1660 but some Puritans continued to regard Christmas festivities as sinful.

Our Christmas customs have developed and changed over the years. The Christmas morning service remains a linchpin for many and is perhaps a relic of the time when the Catholic Church ordered that there should be three Eucharists or masses on Christmas Day – at midnight, dawn and late morning. For many people, the climax of the day is the family Christmas dinner. In many countries the main course is roast turkey. This was not always the case, because until the sixteenth century there were no turkeys in Europe. In those times, people used to have pork or a roast goose or even roast peacock. Even in the nineteenth century, when Charles Dickens wanted to portray the most desirable Christmas dinner in *A Christmas Carol*, its centrepiece is a goose:

> There never was such a goose. Bob said he didn't believe there ever was such a goose cooked. Its tenderness and flavour, size and cheapness, were the themes of universal admiration. Eked out by apple sauce and mashed potatoes,

it was sufficient dinner for the whole family; indeed, as Mrs Cratchit said with great delight (surveying one small atom of a bone upon the dish), they hadn't ate it all at last! Yet everyone had had enough, and the youngest Cratchits in particular, were steeped in sage and onion to the eyebrows!

In this description of the meal Scrooge provided for the Cratchit family, Dickens did much to establish the lasting pattern for Christmas dinner in which the main course is followed by Christmas pudding – traditionally steamed in a cloth in the copper bath in which the family washing was done:

A great deal of steam! The pudding was out of the copper. A smell like a washing-day! That was the cloth. A smell like an eating-house and a pastrycook's next door to each other, with a laundress's next door to that! That was the pudding! In half a minute Mrs Cratchit entered – flushed, but smiling proudly – with the pudding, like a speckled cannon-ball, so hard and firm, blazing in half-a-quartern of ignited brandy, and bedecked with Christmas holly stuck into the top. Oh, a wonderful pudding!

The Christmas pudding dates back several hundred years to the time when there was no fresh fruit to be had at this season of the year and when sugar was an expensive luxury. People then started making special puddings out of spices and dried fruits (like raisins) and nuts – the ingredients of the modern Christmas pudding. Mince pies, containing a similar mixture, are said to have originated as symbols of the manger, their tops being made in the pattern of a hay-rack.

# New Year's Day

*Although New Year's Day is a significant date in the secular calendar and in popular folklore, it has never been regarded as a major festival by the Church and there is only peripheral mention of it in the Anglican liturgy.*

For schools and colleges, the year begins in September – a custom that dates back to the Middle Ages. In medieval times, university students (many of whom actually came from quite poor families) had to return home during the summer months to help with the vital task of harvesting. Only when the harvest was over could they return to their studies and so the start of the September term became recognized as the start of the academic year.

Late September is also the time of Rosh Hashanah, the Jewish New Year. Some Hindus celebrate New Year at this time (though, for others, it is a spring festival). For the Chinese, New Year's Day comes in late January while for Muslims, who use a 48-week calendar based on the cycles of the moon, the New Year festival (known as Al-hijra) steadily moves forward through the western calendar by four weeks each western year. But even in those parts of the world with their own New Year observances, 1 January is a significant day in the calendar.

Despite this widespread observance, it is a seemingly arbitrary date. Unlike the Jewish, Muslim or Chinese New Year Days, it is not related to any phase of the moon. Nor is it related to the winter solstice or 'shortest day' or to the celebration of any important event. To understand why the year should begin on this day, it is necessary to go back to the time of Cleopatra and of one her court astrologers, called Sosigenes. He was consulted by Julius Caesar to see what could be done to standardize the length of each year. His proposal was that future years should each have 365 days, with a leap year every fourth year in February except in centennial years. This pattern became known as the Julian calendar – and years were numbered from the founding of Rome.

This secular scheme did not satisfy the developing Christian Church as it gradually increased in power. It was a monk named Dionysius Exiguus or 'Denis the Little' from southwest Russia who initiated our present numbering of the years. Through what he thought was careful calculation, he deduced that it was then 532 years from the birth of Christ. In this way he created the *anno domini* system, numbering the years 'AD' from the nativity. His calendar nevertheless preserved the Roman months.

As we said in a previous chapter, by the fourth century, Christmas was being observed on 25 December. By the seventh century AD, the Church was also observing that date as the start of the new year. Several centuries later, it was decided that, if the start of the year really was to mark the anniversary of the arrival of Christ on earth, then it should be celebrated nine months earlier, on 25 March – the date of the Annunciation and therefore the beginning of Mary's pregnancy.

From at least the twelfth century onwards, therefore, each new civil calendar year was deemed to begin on 25 March – even though the Church was by now regarding Advent Sunday as the start of its liturgical year. Further change occurred in 1582. Astronomers then advised the Pope (Gregory XIII) that, centuries earlier, Sosigenes had miscalculated the length of the year by approximately 0.0078 of a day. To correct this error, the Pope proclaimed that ten days would 'go missing' and 5 October 1582 would become 15 October 1582. To prevent any future errors, while the centennial years (1700, 1800, etc.) would remain as 'non-leap years', centennial years exactly divisible by 400 (1600, 2000, 2400, etc.) would become leap years.

Roman Catholic countries quickly adopted this new 'Gregorian' calendar (with 1 January as New Year's Day) but an early form of Europhobic resistance swept through the northern and generally Protestant countries. England in particular (where popish plots were disturbing the reign of Elizabeth I) wanted nothing at all to do with what was seen as a Roman 'theft' of ten days. Gradually, however, the rest of Europe drifted into line with Rome. German Protestants and the Swiss, for example, adopted the Gregorian calendar in 1700. Scotland, possibly to annoy England, had adopted it as early as 1600. The consequence of that decision resulted in calendars then helpfully showing different dates in London and Edinburgh. If you travelled south from Edinburgh to London before 25 March, you would arrive a year earlier.

Eventually, in 1750 (by when Sosigenes' error amounted to eleven days), England decided to conform. The Calendar (New Style) Act of 1750 ruled that the day following 2 September 1752 should be 14 September 1752. Only then was 1 January adopted as New Year's Day in England and in what were then its colonial territories such as North America. Russia did not conform until 1917. Unconnected with all this, 1 January has, however, had a minor part to play in the Church's calendar – simply because it occurs a week after Christmas Day.

Eight days after their birth, Jewish boys are circumcised. The event always takes place on that day (unless the baby is too weak), even if it is the Sabbath. According to the Jewish books of law, the Torah, this custom began with Abraham and a man is not considered a Jew unless he is circumcised:

it is a physical sign of membership. It is therefore an important family occasion, and during it the boy is also given his name. As St Luke's Gospel makes clear, Jesus underwent the ceremony one week after his birth – an event the Church consequently commemorates on 1 January. The Church of England Book of Common Prayer names the day simply as 'The Circumcision of Christ'. In recent times it has been usual to give it the additional or alternative title of 'The Naming of Jesus'.

For one branch of the Christian Church, the New Year has, however, had a more distinctive importance. Comparatively soon after John Wesley founded the Methodist movement within the Church of England, Methodists were holding their annual Covenant Services on New Year's Day. These services were established in 1762 but were removed to the more convenient first Sunday of the new year in 1778. Since that date Methodists, and more recently members of other denominations, have joined together to renew their covenant relationship with God. The emphasis of the whole service is on God's readiness to love in return for the acceptance of his love. The covenant is not simply a 'one-to-one' bargain: it is an act made by the whole worshipping community, including the traditional words of the covenant itself:

> I am no longer my own, but yours. Put me to what you will ... put me to doing, put me to suffering ... I freely and whole-heartedly yield all things to your pleasure and disposal ...

Some people have questioned this wording, considering God does not put people to 'suffering', and an alternative wording is now provided. The service also includes Holy Communion and 'should be regarded as the principal service' of the day.

In a way, the Covenant Service has the same theme as

many purely secular new year customs such as first-footing (being the first to enter a Scottish home on New Year's Day). The majority of these customs are a way of putting the past behind us and (depending on your beliefs) trusting in either God or good luck for the coming months.

# The Epiphany

*The Feast of the Epiphany celebrates the visit of the Wise Men to the infant Jesus: his first 'showing' or manifestation to non-Jews.*

She is old, she wears tattered, shabby clothes, she is called 'La Befana' and she is a kind of good fairy. In Italy, many children believe she visits their homes on the twelfth night after the birth of Jesus: 5 January. If they have been good, she will leave them presents of toys or sweets. If they have been naughty, all she leaves is a lump of coal or a heap of dust. So before they go to bed, they hang up a stocking, hoping, of course, that next morning they will find more than coal dust.

Her connection with the Feast of the Epiphany (6 January) results from the legend that she was sweeping her house when the Wise Men went past on their way to find the infant Jesus. She was too busy to pay any attention to them but said she would see them on their way back. But then, of course, they went home another way – and so she never saw them. Ever since, she has been trying to make up for this by giving people presents herself. Often, a grown-up will dress up and pretend to be la Befana (in the way that adults dress up as Santa Claus). When Italian children see this person they call out, '*Ecco la Befana!*' ('Here comes la Befana!'). Her name comes from the word 'Epiphany' which in turn comes from a Greek word meaning 'appearance' or 'showing'. We should therefore, correctly, speak of *the* Epiphany rather than merely 'Epiphany'.

In Russia, a similar legend is told about an old woman called Baboushka. In this tale, the Wise Men visited Baboushka (who lived all alone in a forest) on Christmas Eve. They asked her to travel with them to see the new-born king, and she said she would follow the next day. But by then, she did not know which way to go. Since then, so the story goes, she too has journeyed through the countryside every Christmas – giving presents to children, rather like a 'Mother Christmas'.

Popularly, the Epiphany is equated with Twelfth Night, as *The New Oxford English Dictionary* explains – but that same dictionary adds a further definition of Twelfth Night: 'Strictly, the evening of 5 January, the eve of the Epiphany and formerly the twelfth and last day of Christmas festivities' – which is why many people take their Christmas decorations down that night. The confusion over which day is actually the twelfth day of Christmas stems from the debate whether, when counting the twelve days, you say Christmas Day is the first day or whether you start counting the days from the day after Christmas Day.

Historically, however, Twelfth Night was observed on the evening of 5 January. This was a time of rumbustious merry-making, the celebrations apparently dating back to the 'Saturnalia' of Roman times, which was a week-long feast of debauchery. The law courts and schools were closed, trading ceased and no criminals were punished. The medieval Church harnessed this period of indulgence, naming it the 'Feast of Fools'. A special Twelfth Night cake was baked in which was hidden a bean. In cathedral cities, the chorister who found the bean in his piece of cake was elected the bean king – and was king for the day while those attending his feast joked about things normally held sacred. In England, this custom ceased with the Reformation and its place was taken at the court of Queen Elizabeth I by 'Twelfth Night festivities', held on 6 January.

The programme of events began in the morning. The Queen and her entire court attended chapel and she made a token offering of the three Epiphany gifts: gold, frankincense and myrrh. The present Queen still does this at a royal chapel in St James's Palace in London. The gold is later changed into money and given to the poor, the frankincense is used in church and the myrrh is given to a hospital. In Queen Elizabeth I's time, the religious ceremony was always followed by a banquet and entertainment – for which Shakespeare's play *Twelfth Night* was originally conceived.

For the Christian, the Epiphany (a major holy day) is not only a commemoration of the visit of the Wise Men to Bethlehem but (since they are regarded as the first non-Jews to pay homage to Jesus) is thought of as the 'manifestation' of Christ to the Gentiles and as a sign that his message was to be for all peoples. In reality, the only accepted Gospel to record their visit, that of St Matthew, tells us very little about the Wise Men. All we know for sure is that they came from the east, following a star and searching for a new king. Naturally, they went to the capital city, Jerusalem, and asked the existing ruler King Herod to see 'he who is born king of the Jews'.

Herod obviously needed telling by his own priests and wise men of the prophecy that a king would be born in the little town of Bethlehem. Then follows the familiar story of how he spoke 'privately' to the Wise Men, telling them to find the new king and to report back with their findings. On reaching Bethlehem, the Wise Men gave the Christ Child their presents: gold (a symbol of kingship), frankincense (a symbol of priesthood) and myrrh which foretold suffering. Being warned in a dream of Herod's evil intent, they left the country 'by another way'. And that is all Matthew tells us.

There have been various explanations of the star: it was a comet, a conjunction of two planets, the birth or death of a star or even an early sighting of the then unknown planet

Uranus. It is only in the Gospel of St James (which, of course, did not make its way into the New Testament) that it is described as 'bright' – but an unknown object in the heavens would not have to be bright to excite the interest of astrologers such as the Wise Men. (The distinction between astrology and astronomy did not exist until the sixteenth century.)

We know little else about them for certain. They were not kings: the Greek word *magi* is the plural of *magu*, a wise man. We deduce there were three from the three presents. The likelihood is that they came from Mesopotamia (now Iran, Iraq and Saudi Arabia) and their journey took between ten and twenty days since a fully laden camel can travel over fifty miles a day. Their identification with kingship stems from verses in Psalms 68 and 72 which refer to kings bringing gifts. It was the English historian Bede who suggested they were descended from Noah's three sons with one coming from Asia, one from Africa and one from Europe. In Syria, they acquired the names Larvandad, Harmisdas and Gushnasaph. In western tradition, they became known as Melchior, Caspar and Balthazar. A fourteenth-century book of travel writing ascribed to Sir John Mandeville states that one was a black Ethiopian, and from the fifteenth century onwards one has regularly been depicted in art as being black.

Nowadays we may not wait until Twelfth Night to place the figures of the Wise Men in our Christmas cribs; and to prevent the Epiphany from becoming a neglected, poorly-attended midweek festival, some churches now choose to celebrate it on the nearest Sunday. Although much of the popular story may be legend rather than fact, the truth of this important festival remains: it is a celebration of the universality of the Incarnation.

# *Week of Prayer for Christian Unity*

*Christians around the world join in this annual week of ecumenical prayer for unity, which is normally held from 18 to 25 January.*

For pessimists, it is a scandal that Christians cannot achieve unity. After two thousand years, they point to the divisions and dissent that still exist between the various branches of the Church. For optimists, the second half of the twentieth century was a period in which huge strides were made towards unity, a movement that continues today.

In the past, divisions have resulted in savage butchery. Protestants have burned Catholics, Catholics have killed Protestants. Western and Orthodox Christians cannot even agree about the date of Easter, and tensions (stemming from differing beliefs) continue to result in conflict in various parts of the world. But so much has been achieved, especially at a parochial level, that it is sometimes difficult to remember that until the Second Vatican Council (1962–65) Roman Catholic priests were officially forbidden even to say the Lord's Prayer with Protestants.

Although there were proposals for prayers for Christian unity as early as 1840, it was in the early years of the twentieth century that the movement for unity developed a real momentum. In 1907, an Episcopalian priest in the United

States, Father Paul Wattson, proposed a week or 'Octave of Prayer' for union between Anglicans and Roman Catholics. It was he who chose the dates, namely 18 January (then observed by Roman Catholics as the Feast of Peter's Chair) to 25 January, widely celebrated as the Feast of the Conversion of St Paul. For Wattson, unity meant reunion with Rome, and in 1909 he and the community of Franciscans of whom he was the leader entered into communion with Rome. By 1916, the Octave was being observed by the whole Roman Catholic Church.

In the early 1930s, the idea of working and praying for Christian Unity was taken up by the Abbé Paul Couturier of Lyon in France. Born in 1881, he was a priest and schoolmaster. His interest in ecumenism had developed in the 1920s while working with Russian refugees and, in 1933, he initiated in Lyon a three-day period of prayer for unity. He accepted Paul Wattson's ideas but felt they needed to be broadened into a desire for a more embracing unity. 'We must pray not that others may be converted to us but that we all be drawn closer to Christ.' In 1936, the Octave of Prayer was relaunched as the Week of Universal Prayer of Christians for Christian Unity, to be observed annually in January, on the same dates as the original Octave. This wider concept was approved by Pope John XXIII in 1959 and its title was subsequently abbreviated to the present more manageable one.

The week is now planned jointly by the World Council of Churches and a Vatican council for Christian unity. Annually, they appoint a region to devise the theme and choose readings for the coming year. After local churches in that region have done so, there is a central editing process and then the theme and prayers are handed down to the various participating countries where they can be adapted for local use. In the United Kingdom, the week is organized by Churches Together in Britain and Ireland.

In some parts of the world the week is kept around Pentecost.

# *Candlemas*

*Originally a pagan festival marking the midpoint of winter, halfway between the shortest day and the spring equinox, it came to be a Christian festival of light celebrating the Presentation of Christ in the Temple.*

In the commercial world, Christmas is over by Boxing Day. In many homes, it lasts until the twelfth day of Christmas. Traditionally, however, Christmas (like Lent and Easter) extended for a full forty days – until 2 February, the feast known variously as Candlemas, the Presentation of Christ in the Temple and the Purification of the Blessed Virgin Mary. Both these latter names derive from one of the few recorded episodes in the life of the young Jesus. Forty days after a Jewish boy was born, it was the custom for his parents to take him to the Temple in Jerusalem (if they possibly could) to 'present' or show him to God in thanksgiving for his safe birth: 'Every male that opens the womb shall be called holy to the Lord.' There was also a service of purification or blessing for the mother – hence the two names for the day on which we remember these events.

In the Welsh border country, after the Christmas greenery and other decorations were removed on this day, a bowl of snowdrops was often brought indoors as a 'white purification' although snowdrops in the house at any other time were considered bad luck. Snowdrops are sometimes called Candlemas Bells or Purification Flowers.

On the day that Mary and Joseph took Jesus to the Temple, they met the prophetess, Anna, and a 'righteous' man called Simeon. It was on seeing the infant Jesus that he uttered the words we know as the *Nunc Dimittis*: 'Lord, now lettest thou thy servant depart in peace.' There are echoes of the Presentation in a Nottinghamshire tradition. In the village of Blidworth, on the Sunday nearest to Candlemas, an old wooden rocking cradle, decked with flowers and greenery, would be placed in the candle-lit chancel near the altar. The boy-baby most recently baptized would be laid by the vicar in the cradle and blessed during the service, before being returned to his parents.

In the *Nunc Dimittis*, Simeon is quoted as saying that Jesus will be 'a light to lighten the Gentiles' – which is one reason the day is associated with candles. In many churches around the world, candles are lit and carried in procession as a reminder of this belief that Christ is a guiding light in the darkness of the world. Perhaps because of this association, it used to be the custom for all the candles that were to be used in the church during the coming year to be brought into church and blessed on this day – and so it came to be called the festival day (or 'mass') of the candles.

In Scotland, children would bring money to school on this day to buy candles for the classroom. Later this developed into the bringing of gifts for the schoolmaster himself, with the boy bringing the largest gift being appointed Candlemas King. He reigned for six weeks with certain privileges including being able to cancel punishments. A more widespread domestic custom associated with the day was the lighting of a special candle in the evening. The family would then sit around talking and drinking mulled wine and children were allowed to stay up for as long as the candle burned.

But, like so many Christian festivals, Candlemas was built upon a pagan one. Known as the 'Feast of Lights', this midway point between winter and spring was celebrated for the increasing strength of the life-giving sun – with candles symbolizing the sun. Indeed, in parts of Europe, this day was a fire festival celebrated with bonfires and feasting (like May Day Eve). Such fires were often seen as a defence against cattle disease. The belief that candles give protection against plague, illness and famine lasted much longer.

One of the older pieces of folklore associated with the day is the belief that it predicts the weather for the rest of the winter. If Candlemas Day is sunny and fine (so it is said) there is bad weather to come, but if Candlemas Day is wet and cold then the worst of the winter is over. A similar story exists in Germany. 'On Candlemas Day, the badger wakes up from his winter sleep and peeps out of his hole. If he finds it is snowy, he decides it is time to end his hibernation because he knows that winter is nearly over. But if he finds the sun is shining, he goes back into his hole for he knows there will be more wintry weather yet to come.' The story is much the same in the United States of America, where a ground hog (or woodchuck) rather than a badger is said to forecast the weather.

# Carnival

*This period of feasting immediately precedes Ash Wednesday, the start of the penitential season of Lent, and is known by a variety of names around the world.*

In the West Indies, especially on the island of Trinidad, people begin their preparations for Carnival at the start of the year. They design and make elaborate costumes for the street parades that form a major part of the celebrations, and compose special calypsos. Each year, one of these is selected as that year's carnival song. The start of the two-day carnival, very early on the Monday morning, is called 'Jouvay' (from the French, *Le jour est ouvert*: 'the day is open'). On the Tuesday, people appear on the streets in their costumes, steel bands play, there are fireworks and the feasting and dancing continue until midnight.

Even bigger carnival processions take place in Rio de Janeiro in Brazil where the festival lasts for three days and the traditional music is the samba. Different groups (called 'schools') participate and each group spends a great deal of money on costumes and on the decorated floats which form the various processions. For the poor of Rio, Carnival is a time to forget troubles and to be merry. In Italy too, especially in Venice and a town called Viareggio, and in southern Germany there is also much feasting and drinking. People wear fancy dress and masks and go to parties or join in street parades. In Britain we celebrate by tossing a mixture of eggs, flour and milk in the air.

The word 'carnival' comes from the Italian *carnevale*, *carne* meaning 'meat' and *vale*, 'farewell' – so 'carnival' means 'goodbye to meat' until the fast of Lent is over. But, historically, Lent required abstinence not only from meat but from all animal produce including dairy products. That meant that, on the Tuesday before the fast, anything which would not keep for the forty days of Lent (in the time before freezers or refrigerators) had to be eaten up in order to prevent unnecessary wastage. In French-speaking countries, this resulted in the day being called *Mardi Gras* (literally, 'Fat Tuesday'). In Germany it is *Fasching* or *Fastnacht* (fasting night). The traditional English name of Shrove Tuesday reflects another custom. The word 'shrove' comes from the medieval verb 'to shrive' (to hear confession and to forgive sins) and from a period when it was commonplace to attend confession that day in readiness for Lent which begins the following day, Ash Wednesday.

The custom of shriving dates back to around the year 1000. A sentence in an Anglo-Saxon document entitled *Ecclesiastical Institutes* states: 'In the week immediately before Lent everyone shall go to his confessor and confess his deeds and the confessor shall so shrive him as he then may hear by his deeds what he is to do (in the way of penance).' In former times, Shrovetide lasted for four days, beginning on Shrove Saturday, over Shrove Sunday, Collop Monday and ending with Shrove Tuesday. Collop Monday was so called because people, especially in the north of England, cooked and ate collops on this day, collops being slices of meat or bacon. Schoolchildren often gave their teachers gifts of collops on that day.

Throughout Britain, people developed the habit of using up (before Lent began) any animal fat and also their eggs and milk (animal and dairy products) by making pancakes. Even today, Pancake Day is widely observed by frying and tossing pancakes, and in some towns and villages pancake races are held. These usually start with the ringing of a bell and then the contestants run along the main street, tossing pancakes in a frying pan as they go. There has been one such race at Olney in Buckinghamshire since 1445, from the market square to the parish church. Its origin is uncertain but one legend suggests that a distracted housewife, on hearing the shriving bell calling the faithful to confession, rushed off to the church still clutching her frying pan containing a pancake.

At Olney, the race is started by a churchwarden who rings the large bronze 'Pancake Bell' normally on display in the local museum. Competitors toss their pancakes and then run the 400-metre course. Any woman aged 18 or over may take part, provided she has lived in Olney for at least three months prior to the event, and she must wear the traditional costume of the housewife, including a skirt, apron and head covering. She need not be married. At the finish the winner is required to toss her pancake again before being greeted with the Kiss of Peace and the words 'The peace of the Lord be always with you' spoken by the vicar. Competitors, officials, townsfolk and visitors then attend the Shriving Service in the parish church with competitors placing their frying pans around the font. In 1950, Olney was challenged by the town of Liberal in Kansas in the United States, where they were starting a similar custom, and the two towns now compete annually, the separate races being run on a timed basis.

A more gruesome explanation of 'Pancake Day' dates from Saxon times. A settlement at Linby in Yorkshire was invaded by Danes and the local men fled. The women left behind planned to massacre the Danes on Ash Wednesday, using kitchen knives. As a pledge to take part in the conspiracy, the women agreed to make pancakes the day before. The smell attracted the Danes, who ate and then slept. In the small hours of Ash Wednesday, the women stabbed their unwanted visitors – and annual commemorations of their victory slowly spread to other areas.

In many towns, Shrove Tuesday has also been a day for 'wide games'. Imagine a game of football with few rules and no boundaries to the playing area. All the fit men and youths of the town would take part and the goals might be three miles apart. All you had to do was get the ball into the other team's goal using any method you liked: carrying it, kicking or throwing it, fighting the other team, even pushing your opponents into any handy river. One place where it survives is Ashbourne in Derbyshire. It is a rough, tough and dirty game, in which anyone can compete. The town splits in half, those born north of a local brook being known as the Up'ards, and those born south, the Down'ards. There may be somewhere in the region of 2,000 players.

Very different from a Latin American carnival, it nevertheless serves a similar purpose: the release of energy before the restraints of Lent.

# *Ash Wednesday and Lent*

*Ash Wednesday is the first of the forty days of Lent, the period in the year that both recalls the forty days Christ spent being tempted in the wilderness at the start of his ministry and serves as a preparation for Easter.*

Wearing sackcloth and ashes used to mean what it says. In ancient times, when you wanted to show acknowledgement of, and repentance for, your wrong-doing, then you wore sackcloth and covered yourself in ashes. The legacy of this tradition is the tiny smudge of ashes some Christians receive on their foreheads on Ash Wednesday as a sign of their unworthiness.

In churches where this tradition is maintained, the priest first burns the palm crosses that have been kept from the previous year's Palm Sunday. Experienced priests do this by placing them on a baking tray in a hot oven for a short while – though even this method can result in a lingering acrid smell. The ashes of these crosses are mixed with holy water or oil to make a kind of greyish paste. Then, usually at a Holy Communion service on Ash Wednesday, the priest dips a thumb in the paste and uses it to make the sign of the cross on each person's forehead, saying the traditional words: 'Remember, you are dust and unto dust you shall return.' In many churches, another form of words is now used, such as: 'Turn away from sin and believe in the gospel.'

At the end of the service, some worshippers leave church

with the mark still showing as a sign that they are carrying the cross into the world. Others remove it, either to indicate that (by the end of the service) they have received forgiveness and have been cleansed of their sins or because Jesus told his followers not to show the world when they were fasting.

The custom almost certainly dates from the eighth century. An Anglo-Saxon teacher, Ælfred, wrote: 'Let us do this little at the beginning of our Lent that we strew ashes upon our heads to signify that we ought to repent of our sins during the Lenten fast.' The practice may well owe something to Jewish customs. At a number of points in the Old Testament, there is mention of a mourner covering himself with ashes (or dust). It is certainly a reminder that, according to Genesis, God created us from dust and that 'to dust we shall return'. Because the mark is made in the shape of a cross, it is however also a reminder of baptism and of Christ's sacrifice on the cross as atonement for our sins.

In Latin, the day is called quite explicitly *dies cinerum* or 'day of ashes'. The English word for Lent is derived from the Old English *lencten* which simply meant 'springtime' and possibly referred to the lengthening of the daylight. In German, *Lenz* still means spring. The French for Lent, on the other hand, is *carême*; the Italian is *quaresima* – both being derived from the Latin *quadragesima*, meaning forty days. Now little known, this word does however recall the historic names for the three Sundays immediately before Lent, as they were named in the Book of Common Prayer: Septuagesima, Sexagesima and Quinquagesima, which denoted that the Sundays in question were approximately seventy, sixty and fifty days before Easter.

The observance of Lent certainly predates that of Ash Wednesday but its origins are disputed. For the first three centuries of the Church's existence, there was considerable diversity and debate about the practice of fasting before Easter. What we do know is that, in the year 331, St Athanasius (who was Bishop of Alexandria) wrote a pastoral letter to his people instructing them to observe a period of forty days of fasting before the stricter fast of Holy Week.

This, of course, raises the question as to when is Lent. Many people will immediately answer that it lasts from Ash Wednesday until the Saturday just before Easter Sunday – a day which is properly called Holy Saturday and not Easter Saturday. This actually spans a period of forty-six days but, so this argument goes, as Sundays are always considered festivals (since they mark the resurrection of Christ) they do not count towards the forty days of Lent. Others follow Athanasius in saying Lent lasts the forty days from Ash Wednesday until Palm Sunday – when the stricter observances of Holy Week begin.

Gradually, the observance of 'forty fasting days' became general throughout Christendom. In some churches, especially in Russia and Greece, Lent is still known as the Great Fast. Some say the number forty reflects the hours Jesus spent in the tomb or that it represents the forty years the Israelites were wandering the desert. Much more commonly, it is said to mark the forty days Jesus stayed in the wilderness or desert just before he started his work of teaching and healing. During that time, as we read in the Gospels of St Matthew and St Luke, he fasted and was tempted by the devil.

In olden times, people used to fast quite strictly during Lent – as Jesus did in the wilderness. Roman Catholic authorities stated that fasting meant eating just one full meal in twenty-four hours, while totally abstaining from meat. But how much you ate at that one meal was never prescribed. Indeed, they sound quite lenient: 'Whosoever ... eats a hearty or sumptuous meal in order to bear the burden of fasting satisfies the obligation of fasting.' It was Pope Gregory, writing to St Augustine of Canterbury, who laid down the rule that fasting meant not only abstention from meat but also 'from all things that come from flesh, as milk, cheese and eggs' – hence our Shrovetide customs. In more recent centuries, Roman Catholic authorities permitted the eating of an additional light breakfast on fasting days. Gradually the number of strict fasting days has been reduced, and for many Catholics, and indeed non-Catholics, Good Friday is now the one day on which meat is never eaten.

In those churches where vestments are worn and where the altar frontals and other hangings reflect the liturgical colours of the year, those used in Lent will be either purple (the colour of penance) or made of hessian representing sackcloth. Few Christians now observe a strict Lenten fast but many, as a matter of self-discipline, try to give up some food – maybe chocolate or alcohol. In recent years, many preachers have recommended that Lent is not observed 'negatively' but as a time for doing some positive good in society. Most of all, just as Jesus was tested by his time in the wilderness, so believers try to use the forty days of Lent as a period to strengthen themselves.

# World Day of Prayer

*The World Day of Prayer, held on the first Friday in March, is a worldwide movement. Organized by Christian women from many traditions and from 170 countries, it is observed as a common day of 'informed prayer and prayerful action'.*

The origins of what is widely known as the Women's World Day of Prayer but is properly named simply the World Day of Prayer were laid in the nineteenth century in the United States and in Canada. A number of movements, initiated by women, were then encouraging the greater involvement of women in both home and overseas missionary work. These included the founding of women's boards for missions through which they could work specifically to help women and children.

As early as 1812, women had been encouraging one another to take a leadership role in communal prayer to support this missionary work. This led to a number of separate days or weeks of prayer. In 1887, Presbyterian women started an annual Day of Prayer for Home Missions. In the same year, Methodist women called for a week of prayer and self-denial to aid foreign missionary work. A Baptist Day of Prayer for the latter purpose began in 1891. Six years later, the women of six denominations formed a joint committee to organize a united day of prayer for home missions.

Following the horrors of the First World War, many

women's movements began to link prayers for world peace with their missionary endeavours – and to urge an even more united stance. Within a comparatively short time, representatives of various Canadian women's missionary societies formed a committee which organized the first national Day of Prayer in Canada. That was observed on 9 January 1920. Meanwhile, a similar movement in the United States organized a joint day of prayer for missions on the first Friday in Lent in the same year.

Soon the forms of service devised for these days were gaining a wider distribution and in 1927 there was issued a 'call to prayer' for what was now officially known as the World Day of Prayer for Missions. A 1928 conference held in Jerusalem agreed that worldwide participation would be a bond of unity among women, and the first World Day of Prayer service to be written by a non-American was devised by Helen Kim from Korea in 1930.

Out of this evolved the present World Day of Prayer. An international committee, first convened in 1968, now meets every four years to share feedback and to select themes and choose the national committees that will write the orders of service for future 'days'. These are planned for some eight years ahead.

Although the organizers emphasize that 'all people are welcome', it is often seen as a day especially for women to affirm their faith and to share their hopes, fears, joys and needs. As the international committee expresses it,

> Through World Day of Prayer, women are encouraged to become aware of the whole world and no longer live in isolation; to be enriched by the faith experience of Christians of other countries and cultures; to take up the burdens of other people and pray with and for them – and to become aware of their talents and use them in the service of society.

# *Mothering Sunday*

*This 400-year-old observance, now more commonly known as Mother's Day, occurs on the middle Sunday of the penitential season of Lent. Sometimes named Refreshment Sunday, it came to be regarded as a break in this period of fasting.*

As winter ends and spring approaches, the card shops are suddenly full of Mother's Day cards. Advertisements in the supermarkets encourage children and indeed adults to buy boxes of chocolates and bunches of flowers to give as presents to their mothers. But, properly speaking, Mother's Day does not occur until the month of May.

Mother's Day was first celebrated in 1907. An American woman named Anna Jarvis living in Philadelphia had recently lost her mother. She felt that one day in the year should be set aside for people to honour their mothers. Her idea rapidly became popular and, in 1914, the American government made it an official observance. Since then the second Sunday in May has been called Mother's Day. It is also observed that day in Canada and Australia and in several other countries. On that day some people wear a red carnation as a sign of thanks for a mother who is alive, a white carnation in memory of one who has died. In Britain, the concept of Mother's Day became amalgamated with the much older observance of Mothering Sunday, celebrated on the fourth Sunday of Lent.

The origins of Mothering Sunday are uncertain but we do know that on this day, three or four hundred years ago, people who lived in villages made a point of going not to their local church but to the nearest big church; to what they regarded as their 'Mother Church'. Alternatively, if it was in walking distance, many would go to worship in their cathedral. So Mothering Sunday came to be the day of the year to give thanks for 'Mother Church'.

For this reason, this Sunday became one of various days around the country for an ancient English custom of 'clipping the church'. The children of the parish would form a circle round their church, link hands and sing a hymn in praise of the church. Such a custom was obviously dependent on a large number of local children attending church. In other places, those taking part would link hands and dance round the church. The custom, possibly pagan in origin, is still observed in some country parishes either on Mothering Sunday, at Easter or Pentecost or during Lammas.

Over the years, Mothering Sunday became a time for children to give thanks for all that a mother does for them. In previous centuries, many girls (sometimes as young as 10) 'went into service' meaning that they left home to work as maids in the homes of the wealthy. Many boys also had to leave home to find work or to be apprenticed to a craftsman. In a time when employers were not obliged to give holidays to their employees, servants and apprentices had very little free time. But on Mid-Lent Sunday they were given leave to return home to visit their mothers. Some of the girls were given a special cake to take as a gift while boys would gather bunches of wild flowers on their way home. So developed the custom of the Mothering Sunday 'posy'.

The cake associated with this day is Simnel cake. It is still made in many parts of England, though its shape and recipe vary from place to place. In Devizes, it is baked in the shape of a star. Elsewhere it is round. Almost always, it is spicy and covered with almond paste or thick marzipan. In Shrewsbury, Simnel cake is eaten at Easter and was traditionally decorated with marzipan eggs – the number of eggs equalling the number of months the girl had been away from home. Others suggest there should always be eleven eggs on the cake, representing the number of faithful apostles. The word Simnel is probably derived from the Latin *simila* meaning a fine white flour used in cake making.

A Latin name for this Sunday is Laetare Sunday, *laetare* meaning 'rejoice'. On this day services in Roman Catholic churches begin with these words from the Bible: 'Rejoice ye with Jerusalem and be glad with her.' So, in the days of the Latin mass, the service on this Sunday began, '*Laetare . . .*' The reason for the theme of joy was the imminence of the Easter feast. On Laetare Sunday, the Pope blesses a special ornament called the Golden Rose. It is made in the shape of a bunch of roses and it is given to a person or persons who have done something to help the Catholic Church.

The sackcloth or purple vestments and hangings used in many churches during Lent may be replaced in some Catholic churches by rose-coloured ones (as happens on Gaudete Sunday during Advent) and flowers are placed on altars. In many more churches, however, children are given small bunches or posies of flowers (perhaps violets or primroses) to take to their mothers. In the secular world, it remains a day for giving cards or presents as 'thank yous' to mothers.

# Lady Day

*Lady Day is a traditional English name for 25 March, the date on which the Church commemorates the 'Annunciation of Our Lord to the Blessed Virgin Mary'. That is, it is the day (exactly nine months before Christmas Day) which marks the archangel Gabriel's visit to Mary to tell her that she is to be the mother of Jesus.*

This day, widely known throughout England as Lady Day (in honour of 'Our Lady Mary') used to be one of the most important days of the year. It was the day on which tenants and farmers paid their taxes and their rent. It was also a holiday and (as we have seen on p. 18) it was, from the Middle Ages until 1752, New Year's Day. The logic of this was that, since the years were numbered *anno domini* (meaning 'in the year of Our Lord'), they should begin on the day that marked the arrival of Christ on earth – in the virgin's womb.

This date almost coincides with the spring equinox: the day on which daylight and night are of equal lengths. Christmas similarly almost coincides with the winter solstice: the shortest day of the year. These two 'markers', along with the summer solstice (the longest day) and the autumnal equinox (when, again, daylight and night time are of equal lengths) naturally divide the year into four quarters. Consequently they are the basis for what are known as the four 'Quarter Days': the days on which accounts were to be settled and when magistrates would visit outlying districts to administer justice. This custom enshrined a deep-rooted principle of English justice: debts and unresolved conflicts must not be allowed to linger on. 'Justice delayed is injustice.' Indeed, when the Barons had King John sign Magna Carta at Runnymede in 1215 one of the main principles embodied into it was the promise: 'To none will we sell, or deny, or delay right or justice.'

Promptness still applies where property rents are concerned. Landlords and owners expect the rent to be paid on time and many commercial rents and payments on leased property are still paid on the four Quarter Days – known in some areas as Rent Days. In England, Wales and Northern Ireland the Quarter Days are linked to adjacent religious festivals: Lady Day, the Feast of St John the Baptist (24 June – i.e. Midsummer's Day), Michaelmas (29 September) and Christmas Day. In Scotland, the Quarter Days are referred to as term days and, until recently, were observed on Candlemas, Whitsunday (traditionally celebrated in Scotland on 15 May), Lammas (observed on 1 August) and Martinmas or St Martin's Day (11 November). Legislation, passed in 1990, specified new dates for Scottish term days: Candlemas (28 February), Whitsun (28 May), Lammas (28 August) and Martinmas (28 November).

When England and Wales finally adopted the Gregorian calendar in 1752 (see New Year's Day, p. 19), eleven days were omitted to correct Roman miscalculations in the precise length of the year. There was a populist outcry, leading to riots on the streets in some cities such as Bristol, with mobs claiming, 'We're being robbed of eleven days of our lives.' By way of appeasement (and to avoid accusations of collecting a whole year's taxes for just 354 days), the government decided that annual taxes due on Lady Day 1753 should be collected eleven days late – on 5 April. Each tax year subsequently ended on the same date, a convention which remained in force when William Pitt introduced the 'temporary' measure of income tax in 1799 and was enshrined in law comparatively recently when the Income and Corporation Taxes Act 1970 confirmed that the British income tax year should continue to end on 5 April. By a circuitous route, therefore, it is the archangel Gabriel who decides the Inland Revenue's accounting dates.

The Annunciation may have been a favourite subject for artists through the centuries but many Protestant traditions have downplayed its celebration, often on the grounds that it adulates Mary at the expense of Christ. The day has, however, long been an important one for Catholics. While it was not observed (so far as we know) until the early years of the fifth century, it was certainly being marked by the end of that century. A synod (or meeting) held in 692 spoke of the feast as one 'universally celebrated' in the western Church. The same synod ruled that it should be a feast-day, even though it might occur in Lent.

The choice of date is, of course, inextricably linked to that of Christmas, though which date was established first is now uncertain. During the early Middle Ages, many fanciful calculations were produced to argue that, as the world was created in spring, the Saviour must also have been conceived around the spring equinox. Various ancient writings additionally claim 25 March as the date of the creation of Adam and of the crucifixion (despite the astronomical evidence which determines the date of Passover). Others even claim this date saw the fall of Lucifer, the near-sacrifice of Isaac and the passing of Israel through the Red Sea.

Whether it is called Lady Day or the Feast of the Annunciation, this date can be said to celebrate 'the beginning of Jesus in his human nature' and serve as a reminder that, through Mary his mother, he is a member of the human race.

# Palm Sunday

*On the Sunday at the start of the week that would include his crucifixion and resurrection, the Christian world celebrates the triumphal entry of Jesus into Jerusalem.*

Palm Sunday is the first day of Holy Week. Its observances all commemorate the events of the day on which Christ was cheered by the crowds as he rode into Jerusalem on a lowly donkey. So, for example, in some German towns and villages, a carved, wooden figure of Jesus seated on a wooden donkey (called a *Palmesel*) was pulled in procession through the village. In some Alpine villages, this procession began on a nearby hilltop (just as Jesus began his journey on a hill outside Jerusalem) with everyone making their way to the church in the middle of the town.

Similar commemorations may have originated in Jerusalem as early as the fifth century; perhaps even as early as the year 378. Around that time, it became the custom for Christians to go to the church built near the site of Golgotha where they held their normal Sunday morning service. They then went to the Mount of Olives where more hymns, anthems and lessons were recited. The procession, with the local bishop representing Jesus, finally reached the Church of the Resurrection – the whole event lasting some six hours.

As Christianity became the established religion throughout the Roman Empire, its emperors developed a custom of distributing palms and small presents to their nobles and to their servants on this day. By the seventh century, it was being marked in Gaul (approximating to modern-day France) by the processing of a large cross decorated with flowers through the streets to the principal church of the town. Perhaps because of this, the day acquired its Latin name *Pascha Floridum* or Flower Easter. Similar names evolved in places as far apart as Germany (*Blumensonntag* or *Blumentag*) and Wales (*Sul y Blodau* – which means Flowering Sunday). In Spain, the day is called *Pascua Florida* – a name which in turn was given to the American state of Florida because it was discovered many years ago on Palm Sunday by Spanish explorers.

In many countries, churches are decorated with big palm branches, to symbolize those that the Jerusalem crowds tore down and waved in celebration of what they expected to be a new leader. In medieval England, where palms were virtually unobtainable, it was common to use willow, box or yew branches. This gave rise to a variety of local or regional names for the day: Willow or Sallow Sunday, Yew or Branch Sunday and even Olive Sunday. In a few places, it became known as Fig Sunday. This name stemmed from the custom of eating figs at this time to commemorate the cursing by Jesus of the barren fig tree on the day following the entry into Jerusalem (as recorded by Mark in the eleventh chapter of his Gospel).

By the late Middle Ages, throughout England, the Palm Sunday procession had become a major event in the liturgical year. Early in the service, St John's account of the entry into Jerusalem would be read. The priest then blessed branches of box, willow or yew (which were called palms) and these were distributed to the people. Led by a plain wooden cross, priests and people then processed out of church, waving their 'palms' and singing anthems. They moved to another cross erected outside the east end of the church. Meanwhile, a silk canopy supported on two poles was prepared. Under it was carried the sacrament, and this second procession moved to meet the first by the churchyard cross where Matthew's account of the triumphal entry was being read. In different places, varying ceremonies were then performed and anthems sung. Eventually, the two processions made their way back to the main church door with the congregation passing under the canopy to re-enter the building. In those churches which possessed a rood screen (a wooden screen separating the nave from the chancel and surmounted by a crucifix), the crucifix would have been veiled for the duration of Lent. Now it was uncovered, as a focus for the coming week's services, and the mass would proceed as normal – but with one exception. For the Gospel, the complete passion story from St Matthew would be sung with the words of Christ taken by a bass voice while a tenor sang the narration.

Puritan reforms in 1548 led to the use of palms being abandoned in England and Wales (as were the use of candles at Candlemas and ashes on Ash Wednesday). Gradually, following the Restoration and again during the Anglo-Catholic revival of the nineteenth century, these were re-introduced. Nowadays, they are quite widespread with the distinctive ceremony of the day being the blessing of palms which are placed on the altar where flowers would ordinarily be. These palms may include both small crosses and larger branches. In many churches they will be sprinkled with holy water or blessed with incense. The smaller crosses are then distributed to the congregation who hold them aloft as they take part in a procession either inside or round the exterior of their church. Brave clergy have sometimes sought the services of a real donkey to lead the way. For the Gospel, it is common practice to read the entire story of the Passion, up to the crucifixion. The Anglican Book of Common Prayer preserved the use of St Matthew's Gospel for this purpose. It is now common to read the different Gospel accounts in successive years and in some churches a number of readers are used to create a dramatic effect – just as happened in medieval times.

The small palm crosses, made out of folded strips of palm, are taken home by the congregation and many keep them in prominent places until the start of the following Lent. In earlier centuries they were also placed in barns and in fields where there were growing crops. Now, as then, they serve as a reminder both of the joy of the first Palm Sunday and of what was to happen on the Friday of that same week.

# *Holy Week*

## *(including Maundy Thursday)*

*Holy Week, the 'heart' of the Christian year, reflects the
events of the days Jesus spent in Jerusalem immediately
before his crucifixion. While being part of a week of
solemn observances and penance, Holy Thursday is also
marked by a succession of ceremonies of a joyful nature.*

During the three days following Palm Sunday, Jesus lived in
the village of Bethany, near Jerusalem. The Gospels tell us he
visited the city each day, teaching and talking to the people
who gathered to hear him in the outer courtyard of the
Temple, but there is some disagreement as to which day
certain events occurred. Others are easier to pinpoint. For example, Wednesday was almost certainly the day on which
Judas bargained with the Jewish high priests to act as their
'spy' and to lead them to a place where they might arrest
Jesus – leading to that day of the week being known in
Ireland as Spy Wednesday.

Once upon a time, the whole Christian world (then almost
synonymous with the western world) observed the week as a
period of fasting and prayer. In the year 329, St Athanasius
of Alexandria spoke of a 'severe' fast maintained for 'those
six holy and great days which are a symbol of the creation of
the world'.

Few now maintain a 'severe' fast; even fewer relate it to the 'six days' of creation; and the week passes with little notice in the secular world: it's simply a shorter than usual working week ending in a holiday weekend. Nevertheless, the faithful still mark the days of Holy Week with services that are solemn in nature and designed to encourage a spirit of repentance in preparation for Easter. These may include prayerful processions following 'the Stations of the Cross' (see p. 62) or late-night services of prayer called Night Prayer or Compline. The latter have their origins in the evening offices (or services) said or sung by monks and nuns. These included a service known as Tenebrae ('Darkness') which has been sung on the Wednesday, Thursday and Friday evenings during Holy Week since the ninth century. Included in the service is the gradual extinction of candles held in a triangular candlestick. The snuffing out of these candles, one by one, symbolizes the desertion of Jesus by his disciples. Eventually, only the topmost candle remains alight, representing Jesus. This is then taken down and hidden behind the altar; a loud noise may be created to indicate his death; the candle is then restored to its place and the congregation departs. In an otherwise unlit chapel or church, it can be a highly dramatic reinforcement of the Easter message.

Like Tenebrae, many of the solemnities of this week are tinged with hope and expectation of the coming resurrection. In some countries, such as Spain and Italy, there are colourful street processions. For example, in the Spanish city of Seville, these are held every evening during Holy Week. Different groups of people take part, each carrying heavy platforms (called *pasos*) on their shoulders. On these platforms are carvings showing scenes from that first Holy Week, including the crucifixion. Some of the wooden figures are dressed in elaborate clothes which reflect their importance. The figure of Mary, the mother of Jesus, is often dressed as a queen but is called the Queen of Pain – because of the anguish she must have suffered that week. All of the *pasos* (there are more than a hundred) are decorated with flowers and candles. They are followed in procession by people dressed in white tunics and black hoods. These are penitents: that is, people publicly demonstrating repentance for their sins.

In some towns at this time of year, people organize 'Passion Plays'. Not only do these plays retell the events of Good Friday, but many also show what happened on the Thursday of the first Holy Week. Known as Maundy Thursday, it is the day on which Jesus had his Last Supper with his twelve closest disciples. Held in an upstairs room in the house of a friend, it was here that he was to give them the 'new commandment' (to love one another). In Latin, the word for commandment is *mandatum* from which is derived the word 'Maundy'.

Before giving them this commandment, Jesus washed the feet of his disciples. In hot countries (such as Palestine) this act was a mark of respect to visitors and intended to make them comfortable after a long journey. The task was usually performed by servants or slaves. That Jesus should do it himself was a way of showing his humility and indicated that following God involves service. Since then it has been customary on Maundy Thursday for popes, monarchs, bishops and priests to wash the feet of the poor. In Rome, the Pope still washes the feet of twelve men and women. In medieval Europe, it was usual for the king to wash the feet of specially invited needy people and then to give them clothes, food and money. The last British monarch to wash the feet of the poor was King James II but the custom of the monarch presenting gifts on Maundy Thursday survives today. During the reign of Elizabeth I, the gifts were of cloth, fish, bread and wine. The cloth was replaced by money in 1725 and the provisions also by money in 1837. Originally, the presentation was made at a chapel in Whitehall but the ceremony was later transferred to Westminster Abbey. From

1688, the monarch no longer performed the task in person until 1932 when the custom was revived by George V. Queen Elizabeth II has made the distribution in most years of her reign and created a tradition of carrying out the presentation in a different cathedral each year. The purses of money are given to the same number of elderly men and women as the age of the king or queen. In fact, they are each given two purses. In one are four specially minted silver coins with face values of one, two, three and four pence. In the other purse is ordinary money for use.

Since the fourth century, there have been special memorials on this day of the institution of the Eucharist (the Greek word means thanksgiving) or Lord's Supper. In Jerusalem, in the early centuries of the Church, this took place in the late afternoon. All communicated and then went to the Mount of Olives to commemorate the agony of Christ in the Garden of Gethsemane with appropriate prayers, readings and hymns, returning home only when Friday dawned.

In the middle of the twentieth century, it again became the custom to commemorate the institution of the Eucharist with an evening Holy Communion service which now sometimes incorporates a symbolic foot-washing ceremony performed by the priest. Since the service is (in large part) a thanksgiving, the purple or sackcloth vestments and hangings are replaced by white ones. For centuries, this service has been followed by the removal of all decorations, hangings and candles from the church, in preparation for the following day of mourning, Good Friday. Often known as 'the stripping of the altars', this was (and often still is) accompanied by the reading or singing of psalms or passages from the prophets or Gospels. In medieval times, each of the 'stripped' altars had wine and water poured upon it and was then cleaned with a broom made of sharp twigs. The symbolism of each act was made clear to the congregation. The stripping of the altar symbolized the stripping of Jesus for crucifixion, the wine and the water were the blood and water that flowed from his side while the broom represented the scourging or the crown of thorns that was pressed upon his head.

Following the service, the consecrated bread and wine are carried solemnly to an 'altar of repose'. This may be a side altar which has been decorated with flowers to represent Gethsemane. Here, a watch or vigil is held as the congregation meditates upon the arrest and impending death of Jesus. Tenebrae might be sung at this point.

One other ceremony associated with Maundy Thursday is the Chrism Mass or Eucharist. Chrism is a mixture of oil and balsam used in some churches at baptism, confirmation and ordination. By tradition, it can be consecrated only by a bishop. In Roman Catholic and many Anglican cathedrals, this is done at a Maundy Thursday morning Eucharist, and the oils are taken by parish priests and ministers for use in their churches during the coming year.

For all these reasons, along with every Sunday, Maundy Thursday is one of the principal holy days of the ecclesiastical year.

# *Good Friday*

*The day which commemorates the crucifixion of Jesus is the most solemn day of the Christian year and is marked by distinctive church services. Until comparatively recently, its significance was widely respected with shops and places of entertainment remaining closed. Now the prevailing atmosphere is much like any other holiday.*

Why the day which marks the death of Jesus should be called 'Good' puzzles many people. A frequent explanation is that, although it is indeed a sorrowful occasion, it is 'good' because the events of that day were necessary for there to be the joy, hope and glory of the resurrection three days later, on the first Easter Sunday morning. In fact, the name 'Good Friday' probably derives from 'God's Friday' which was used in earlier centuries. Even earlier, the Anglo-Saxons called it Long Friday. In Germany it is *der stille Freitag*: Silent Friday.

The silence which prevailed for much of the day in previous times may now have disappeared (for many it is a day devoted to shopping or attending sporting events), but some customs remain. Many who would otherwise never consider fasting eat fish rather than meat on this day. Hot cross buns are still eaten at this time, as they have been since the seventeenth century, although they are now stocked by supermarkets the year round. In the past, however, buns actually baked on Good Friday were supposed to have special qualities. Not only were they thought to bring good luck, but (if they were kept for some time) they were believed to have healing qualities. This may not be complete nonsense: the mould that grows on them is not dissimilar to penicillin.

Older people may recall some of the taboos and super-stitions associated with the day. It used to be considered unlucky to use a hammer and nails on Good Friday. Washing clothes would also bring ill luck. In fact, because the cruci-fixion occurred on a Friday, all Fridays were thought by some to be less than lucky days. This belief is still widespread when Friday is the thirteenth day of the month – the origin of this superstition stemming from the fact that there were thirteen people at the Last Supper. On the other hand, Good Friday was considered a lucky day on which to plant crops, espe-cially potatoes, while those born on the day were said to have the power of seeing and commanding spirits.

For the church-goer, Good Friday is in part a day of mourning. Many services take the form of meditations on Christ's suffering and death on the cross, and their meaning for today's believers. In some towns there are special Good Friday processions of witness, or re-enactments of the cruci-fixion. This is also a time when many choose to make a devotional procession, following the Way of the Cross.

As the Gospels make clear, whenever anyone was con-demned to death in the Roman Empire, he was made to walk to his place of execution. The route believed to be the one Jesus was made to take has since been walked by millions of Christians in memory of what happened to him that Friday. They follow the *Via Dolorosa* (the Way of the Cross, literally 'mournful way') through the narrow streets of the old part of the city. Along it are fourteen places where people stop to remember what happened to Jesus on his journey, these stop-ping points being called stations or the Stations of the Cross. This observance is also practised in many churches on Good Friday (or at other times during Lent or Holy Week), when congregations make their own Way of the Cross, stopping to pray and meditate at fourteen pictures or statues which recall the original Stations of the Cross.

The first station recalls the moment when Jesus was condemned to death. The second marks his being given the crossbeam to carry, while the third is the point where he stumbled and fell for the first time under the weight of the cross. The fourth station represents the spot where, so it is said, he passed Mary his mother as she stood in the crowds. The fifth station is where the Romans seized a man called Simon from Cyrene out of the crowd and made him help Jesus carry the heavy beam. The sixth recalls the moment a woman wiped the sweat and blood from Jesus' face. She is remembered today by the name Veronica – which means 'true icon' since it is believed the image of Christ's face was imprinted as a 'true picture' on the cloth she used. The seventh station is where Jesus fell a second time.

In Jerusalem, the Way now leads out of the old city, through what were its boundary walls to the eighth stopping point, where Jesus spoke to the women of Jerusalem. Next is the ninth station, where Jesus fell for a third time. The tenth station is the Place of the Skull, Golgotha, where Jesus was to be crucified. This spot, and the remaining stations in Jerusalem, are now inside the Church of the Holy Sepulchre. At the tenth station, worshippers remember how he was stripped of his clothes; and at the eleventh, how he was nailed to the beam he had been carrying and then hoisted up onto the cross.

At the twelfth station, they remember his death on the cross three hours later; and at the thirteenth, they recall how his body was taken down from the cross and given to Joseph from Arimathea to be put in a burial place. The last station marks that spot: the place where, it is said, the body of Jesus was laid to rest.

In many churches, the main service on Good Friday takes place between midday and three o'clock (the hours Jesus is said to have hung on the cross), often with pauses or hymns on each hour so that people who are not attending the whole service may arrive or depart. It may take the form of a meditation based on the seven last words of Jesus on the cross, with hymns, prayers and short sermons; or it may incorporate the Stations of the Cross and also the Veneration of the Cross (sometimes known as the Adoration or Proclamation of the Cross).

This liturgy derives from an ancient practice observed in Jerusalem from possibly as early as the fourth century in which Christians venerated what was said to be the 'true cross'. In more recent times, especially in Catholic churches, it takes the form of the gradual unveiling of a cross or crucifix during which a choir may sing verses known as the Reproaches. When the cross is completely unveiled it is placed at the foot of the altar, perhaps on a cushion prepared for it. The priest then bows low and kisses it. Other worshippers may then come forward and bow before it or kiss it. This ceremony, which can be very moving to its participants, became known in England (somewhat dismissively) as 'creeping to the cross' – perhaps because it was regarded by non-Catholics as worship of a graven image. The Catholic would answer that it is not an act of worship but of reverence and prayer before the instrument by which Christ redeemed humankind.

In many cases the Veneration of the Cross is followed by 'the mass of the pre-sanctified'. By tradition, the Eucharist is never celebrated on Good Friday but people may receive Holy Communion in the form of bread and wine consecrated or sanctified at the previous evening's service.

# Easter Eve

*The day between Good Friday and Easter Day is known variously as Easter Eve, Holy Saturday, the Easter Vigil and (in olden times) Grand or Great Saturday. In the secular world it is often wrongly called Easter Saturday. Technically speaking, Easter Saturday occurs at the end of Easter Week. By whatever name it is known, the day is a bridge between the season of penance and the joy of Easter Day.*

The day before Easter Sunday is a day of waiting and expectation, a day of confident preparation and 'certain hope' for the resurrection of Christ. In few places is the vigil celebrated with such intensity as it is in Greece.

Imagine a typical town on, say, the island of Crete. Throughout the Saturday there is a mood of growing excitement. Later, there will be fireworks – although the more impatient boys of the village have been setting some off for several days now, to the annoyance of the older people of the town. As evening comes, the air is still warm and, in the Easter moonlight, the white-painted stone church stands bright against the night sky. Outside the church, the younger men have been building a huge bonfire. That's for later. Now, everyone leaves their homes and the cafés and makes their way to church. They each carry a candle – unlit, despite the fact it is already dark. Quickly the church becomes crowded and not everyone can get inside. The congregation stands as the lights in the building are turned out and Easter hymns are sung. There is a procession and then the priest chants the Gospel story of the first Easter morning: the visit to the cave or tomb and the discovery that the body was no longer there.

As midnight approaches, the priest comes forward from the far end of the church carrying two lighted candles. 'Come and take light,' he says. The people nearest to him light their candles from his and then the other people light their candles in turn, one from another. The darkness gives way to light as more and more candles burn. Soon the light is passed to those who were unable to get in and who are still outside. At midnight, the priest cries out the Easter greeting, '*Christos anesti!*' The Greek words mean 'Christ is risen!' The people shout the reply, '*Alithos anesti!*' ('He is risen indeed!') The congregation hug one another and exchange the same Easter greeting.

By now the bonfire has been lit and, as everyone leaves the church, the fireworks are set off and the bells of the church clang as if to echo the excitement of the people. As the night wears on there is singing and dancing but, gradually, families make their way home, carrying their candles with great care so that they are not extinguished. Those who live farther away go by car but still try to keep their candles alight. Once the candles are home, they are used to light any oil lamps and other candles.

The service emphasizes the Easter message: the darkness and sorrow of Good Friday are followed by light, life and hope. In medieval times, the Easter vigil would have been celebrated in this way throughout much of Europe – and its symbolism was probably all the more intense in the colder, darker northern countries. Before going to church on Easter Eve for 'the new light', people would, as a considerable act of faith, put out all their oil lamps, candles and even the fire in the hearth so that there was no fire or light at all in their home. During the service (as in parts of Greece today), the priest would strike a stone or flint against the wall of the church until it made a spark from which a candle could be lit. And then, again as in Greece today, the people would light their candles from that one candle with the priest saying, 'Father, we share in the light of your glory, through your Son, the light of the World. Make this new fire holy and inflame us with new hope.' After the service, the people would then carry home the new fire of Easter to light and warm their homes.

During the early Middle Ages, Easter vigil services like this were held during the daytime on Holy Saturday, but in recent years have been restored to a more suitable evening timing when they are now held in many Roman Catholic and some Anglican churches. Often they begin outside the church, with the minister or priest striking a flint against the church porch to produce the spark that will light the first candle. More frequently a ready-lit charcoal brazier is used. The service begins with words such as these: 'Brothers and sisters in Christ, on this most holy night, in which our Lord Jesus Christ passed over from death to life, the Church invites her members, dispersed throughout the world, to gather in vigil and prayer.' A very large candle is then lit as a symbol of Christ, the light of the world. This is called the Paschal candle and is marked with a cross, an alpha and an omega (the first and last letters of the Greek alphabet) and the four numbers of the year to symbolize the belief that Christ has, is and always will be with humankind. Paschal is another word for Easter and, like most European names for Easter (for example, the French word *Pâques*, the Spanish *Pascua*, the Dutch *Paach* and the Swedish *Pask*), is derived from the Hebrew *Pesach*, meaning Passover.

Because Holy Saturday was the day on which many Christians were baptized in former times, the modern Easter vigil service often includes a renewal of baptismal vows in preparation for the new life of Easter Day.

# *Easter*

*Easter, the celebration of Christ's resurrection three days
after his crucifixion, is the most important festival of the
Christian year. While it may be of supreme importance
to Christians, it does not now grip the popular imagination in the way that Christmas does. Indeed, its meaning
is often lost in a plethora of chocolate eggs.*

Eggs, chickens, rabbits, flowers . . . Easter is, in the popular
mind, supremely a spring festival. For those who live in the
northern hemisphere, it is hard to imagine it occurring at any
other time of the year. And while it may seem a happy conjunction that the Christian festival of new life and rebirth
should coincide with the season of renewal and new life in
the world of nature, it is also true that this coincidence often
distracts attention from the festival's Christian significance.

Every Sunday is, of course, a commemoration of the resurrection – but since we know that the crucifixion and resurrection happened at the time of the Jewish Passover festival,
we know what time of year it happened: the Sunday after the
fourteenth day of the Jewish lunar month of Nisan. From the
earliest years of the Church (some say since the time of St
Peter and St Paul), this particular Sunday has had a special
importance. But the precise calculation as to which Sunday in
the western calendar should be observed as Easter Day
divided (and still divides) the Church. So far as Rome was
concerned, the date of Easter was determined by the Council

of Nicæa in 325. Here it was decided that it should occur on the first Sunday after the Paschal full moon: that is, the full moon that occurs on the day of the vernal equinox (21 March) or on any of the next 28 days. The Celtic Churches maintained their own observance and only adopted the Roman method of calculation at the Synod of Whitby held in the year 664. Since then, Roman Catholic, Anglican and Protestant churches have observed the festival on the same day – a day that can occur as early as 22 March and as late as 25 April, something which often infuriates the secular world, much of which would prefer a fixed date. Meanwhile, the Orthodox Churches still follow their own calendar which means that only occasionally is Easter observed at the same time in, say, Rome and Athens.

While its name in many European languages stems from the Hebrew *Pesach*, meaning Passover (from which we derive the word 'Paschal'), the English word 'Easter' is of uncertain origin. Many believe (as did the seventh-century monk and historian Bede) that it was borrowed from a pagan spring-time festival known as Ostara, held in honour of the Teutonic goddess of the dawn Eostre. This festival of renewal marked the beginning of spring and also the equinox: the date when the day and the night are of equal length. The dawn goddess was thought always to carry a basket of eggs and to be accompanied by a hare or rabbit. In Germany (and in other countries), young children still expect a visit from Easter Hare or *Oster Hase* who supposedly hides chocolate eggs in gardens, ready to be discovered early on Easter morning.

For Christians, the Easter story is about another form of new life: the triumph of Jesus over death – something first made apparent to Mary Magdalene, who went to his burial place only to find the stone covering its entrance had been rolled away and the tomb empty. Later, other followers (notably Peter and John) made the same discovery, and Mary saw the risen Lord. These events are often commemorated in churches by the construction of an Easter Garden – an echo of the Easter Sepulchre which could be found in every church in the Middle Ages. This might be a permanent or movable feature. If it was the latter, it would often take the form of a wooden frame, decorated with tapestries and carved or painted panels illustrating some aspect of the resurrection.

From the resurrection comes the message of new life and salvation that is central to the Easter morning celebrations, especially in the form of Holy Communion. Indeed, the Church has historically taught that Easter is a 'day of obligation', a day on which all its baptized and confirmed members should receive Holy Communion. In medieval times (and later), receiving Holy Communion at Easter was known as 'taking one's rights' – indicating that receiving or taking Communion was a way of claiming one's place in the adult community.

As Christianity spread through Europe, many pagan customs were adopted and 'Christianized' – possibly to placate local opposition to the 'intruding' faith, possibly as a way of teaching Christian truths. So, for example, the giving of eggs (around the time of what had been Ostara) was maintained, and a custom developed of bringing eggs (forbidden food during Lent) to church on Easter Day to be blessed. For the pagan, the egg was simply a symbol of new life returning to the world after the cold, dead days of winter. For the Christian, however, the egg can be said to resemble the tomb of Jesus. When it breaks, it is like the opening of the tomb.

While chocolate eggs have now widely replaced real ones as Easter gifts, older traditions survive. In Poland at Easter, people take a needle and make a tiny hole at each end of an egg. Then all the contents can be blown out. A pattern is made with wax on the outside of the empty shell. Next, the shell is dipped in bright dye which stains the shell, except where the wax has been. This is done several times with different wax patterns and different dyes to make attractive Easter presents. On Maundy Thursday, many Greeks dye or paint hard-boiled eggs red to signify the blood of Christ. These are baked into twisted sweet-bread loaves or distributed on Easter Sunday.

Many different games are played with eggs at Easter. One game is played in much the same way both in Greece and in parts of northern England. You hold an ordinary hard-boiled egg in your fist and knock it, end on, against your opponent's egg – to see whose is the stronger and whose egg can score most victories. In many districts, Easter is also a time for egg-rolling games – again using hard-boiled eggs, still known as Pace (or Pasch) Eggs in some places. Often these are decorated with different colours and then rolled down hills to see which egg can go the farthest before it breaks. This game is even played on the lawns of the White House in Washington DC on Easter Monday when the gardens are open to the public.

Another Christian symbol especially associated with Easter is the lamb. The origin of this symbol is related directly to the Jewish Passover when Jews traditionally sacrificed a lamb in the course of the festival. For Christians, Jesus became the one necessary sacrifice: the 'Lamb of God' dying on the cross to provide liberation from death through his resurrection. During the Middle Ages roast lamb became the traditional main course of the Pope's Easter dinner, and it is still customarily served on Easter Sunday in many European countries.

One other Easter custom that survived until recent years was dressing up in new clothes for Easter, women choosing their new hat or bonnet with especial care. This may stem from the fact that, since weddings could not take place during Lent, the period immediately following Easter became a traditional time for getting married – which meant a need for new clothes.

# *May Day*

*One of the few pagan feasts never to be successfully Christianized, this major spring fertility festival has (in modern times) become a celebration of the dignity of labour.*

Early in the morning of the first day of May, the sandman goes through the streets of the small Cheshire town of Knutsford, sprinkling coloured sand on the pavements. This is supposed to bring good luck to the houses he passes – especially the homes of those soon to be married. The custom goes back to the time of King Cnut (or Canute), after whom Knutsford is named. He once saw a wedding procession go by and emptied his shoe of sand at the couple's feet, wishing them as many children as there were grains of sand in his shoe.

May Day is carnival time in Knutsford, with processions, morris and maypole dancing, fancy dress parades and the crowning of a girl chosen be 'Queen of the May'. These or similar traditions are preserved in many English towns at this time of year – some being distinctive to certain localities. For example, in Padstow in Cornwall and in Minehead in Somerset, the 'Obby Oss' (a man dressed up as a strange-looking horse) dances through the streets, chasing women and girls.

These may sound like quaint, pleasantly amusing country customs. In fact they (and similar celebrations) date back to the pagan festival of Beltane, also known as May Eve or

Walpurgis Night – a time when a village maiden was chosen as Queen of the May to preside over the festivities. The name Beltane derives from a Celtic word, *bel*, meaning 'fire'. That in turn stems from Belinos, which was one name for the sun god. In the pagan world, Beltane marked the height of spring, the start of summer, and was a time of hope; the antithesis of Samhain (now known as Hallowe'en). Indeed, one Celtic name for Beltane was Cetsamhain (or 'opposite Samhain'). It was, in practice, a time of more or less unbridled sexual activity. Younger couples would go 'a-maying'; which meant spending the night of May Eve (30 April) together in the woods, returning (somewhat rumpled) the next morning to dance round a phallic maypole. Older married couples were permitted to remove their wedding rings that night – and with them the restraints they implied.

The Celts also regarded horses with great respect and believed the May 'oss' brought fertility to the land and to people – hence the Padstow customs. Maypole and morris dancing had similar purposes: the higher the morris dancers jumped, the higher the crops would grow. But a key element of the Beltane celebrations, as its name suggests, was the 'bel fire'. This sacred bonfire was said to have healing and purifying powers and, at the start of the festival, all domestic fires and flames would be extinguished to be re-lit later with brands taken from the bel fire (a tradition which the Church maintained in its Easter Eve liturgy). A Beltane Fire Festival has again been held on Calton Hill in Edinburgh since the mid-1980s.

In medieval times, the Christian Church attempted to counteract these lingering May customs by naming the season Roodmas, an occasion for honouring not the maypole but the rood or cross. Similarly, in Germany, where May Eve was a time when witches were said to be particularly active as they gathered on mountain tops (as portrayed in Goethe's play *Faust*), the Church began to celebrate the day in honour of St Walpurga, an abbess credited with powers against witchcraft. Traditions developed whereby *Walpurgisnacht* (Walpurgis Night) became a time when boys of all ages were allowed to make as much noise as possible as soon as the sun had set – noise being considered a defence against evil spirits.

By the beginning of the nineteenth century, the population of European countries was becoming increasingly urbanized. Not only were workers in the new industries often forced to labour for fourteen hours a day, they were given no paid holidays. There was simply no time to go a-maying. Then, in 1833, a mill-owner called Robert Owen wrote about his vision of a golden age without poverty or injustice. He decided this age should begin on 1 May which he believed should be a 'Festival of Labour'. Over the next fifty years, trade union leaders began to agitate for an eight-hour working day and then, in 1889, leaders of the labour movement from all over Europe met in Paris, and decided May Day should be a day of demonstrations to cut the working day to eight hours. Since then, 1 May has been marked as Labour Day in many industrialized countries, a time for expressing pride in work, solidarity between workers and hope for the future. In 1978, the first Monday in May became a Bank Holiday in England and Wales (as it had been in Scotland for some years before).

Possibly because May Day was widely celebrated in communist countries, the Roman Catholic Church (opposed to communism as it forbade religious teaching) began to feel the need to mark the dignity of honest labour. Following the Second World War, Pope Pius XII declared 1 May to be the Feast of St Joseph the Workman – the earthly father of Jesus and a carpenter. But despite Roodmas and St Joseph, May Day has never really become well known as a Christian holy day.

# Christian Aid Week

*Since 1957, the second week in May has been the prin-
cipal fund-raising week for Christian Aid's development
projects in the Third World.*

Two-thirds of the money raised in Christian Aid Week comes
from house-to-house collections, often organized by local
churches working together in order to cover all the roads and
streets in their locality. Many churches, youth groups,
schools and other organizations have also developed supple-
mentary fund-raising activities ranging from sponsored
walks to cake and plant stalls, car-washing, street collections
and other sponsored events.

Christian Aid came into existence in 1945. Its original
name was Christian Reconciliation in Europe, its purpose
being to address the needs of refugees and churches across
Europe in the aftermath of the Second World War. In 1949 it
became an integral part of the British Council of Churches
and became known as the Department for the Inter-Church
Aid and Refugee Service. Its scope broadened as it became
involved with refugee settlement and justice issues on a
worldwide basis, working closely with the World Council of
Churches.

Its name was finally simplified to Christian Aid in 1964,
following the increasingly high profile of its fund-raising
week (and chief source of income), which had begun seven
years earlier in 1957. Since the reorganization of the World

Council of Churches in 1991, Christian Aid has been a separate legal entity, but remains in close relationship with the WCC.

People give a number of reasons for not supporting charities. 'Money given to charity only gets spent on advertising.' 'The money doesn't reach the people it's meant for.' 'Charities get all the money they need from the Lottery.' 'Christian charities only help Christians.' 'I can't give enough to do any good.' In the case of Christian Aid, most of these can be refuted. Out of every £1 the charity receives, 75p is spent on tackling poverty and 11p on campaigns and education. Just 14p is spent on fund-raising and running the charity. At the 'sharp end' of its work, it uses local churches and other organizations to make sure the money goes where it can do most good and to those who need it most, whatever their beliefs. It is not a missionary society, nor does it take money from the National Lottery. As to the last objection, Christian Aid knows it cannot do enough by itself to end poverty but works to change trade systems and local laws that cause or maintain poverty.

Since its beginnings, Christian Aid has concentrated on long-term development projects where the need is greatest, working with people and communities regardless of race or creed. Today it works in over sixty of the world's poorest countries, its creed being summed up in the statement 'We believe in life before death.' One simple example can stand to illustrate its methods. In Ethiopia, an environment club was set up to teach children at one school how to look after their land. To combat the lack of rain, club members were taught how to dig crescent shapes around banana plants. Rain-water could then collect there and soak in – otherwise it would have run away, eroding the soil. Before the club started, the village had no fruit. Now it grows a variety of fruits and vegetables and is teaching other schools how to do the same.

# *Rogationtide*

*Rogation Sunday is the Sunday before Ascension Day (which occurs forty days after Easter) and the Monday, Tuesday and Wednesday following Rogation Sunday are known as Rogation Days. The word 'Rogation' is derived from the Latin verb* rogare *('to ask'): Rogationtide was (and is) the period when rural communities asked God's blessing on the crops.*

By May, farmers have finished sowing. The seeds of corn and other crops are in the ground, waiting for 'such weather, as that we may receive the fruits of the earth in due season' (to quote a prayer for fair weather in the Book of Common Prayer). And so, for centuries, it was natural at this time of year in a primarily rural economy to ask God's blessing on the crops and to pray for a good harvest later in the year.

Historically, instead of meeting in church, congregations would walk out together to say a prayer in each field. These processions from field to field were accompanied by the ringing of handbells and the carrying of banners and a processional cross – leading to the week being popularly known as Cross Week in some areas. In the minds of medieval congregations, the aim of the procession was not only to invoke good weather and fertility but to drive away evil spirits that might cause division and dispute between neighbours and sickness in cattle and flocks. During the processions, the Litany of the Saints was chanted and the whole procession would halt at what was generally believed to be the finest oak tree in the parish. Here the priest would deliver the Gospel reading. Such trees became known as Gospel Oaks. In some places, the name survives: there is a railway station in north London called Gospel Oak – once a rural location.

They also had another purpose, reflected in another name formerly used for the season: Gang Days. Nothing to do with the modern term 'gang master' (the organizer of cheap, casual labour), it derived from an old word 'ganging' – in turn stemming from a German root *gangen*, meaning 'to go'.

Gang Days were the days for beating the bounds of the parish. In some areas, this was a separate Ascension Day custom, but in many places it was part of the Rogation festivities. Principally, it was an act of demarcation, a way of fixing in everyone's mind exactly where one village (or parish) began and ended: a way of marking its 'bounds' or boundaries. The priest, local dignitaries and nobles all participated and a strong communal spirit was engendered. Accounts survive of incidents where processions from neighbouring parishes happened to meet and come to blows – because one parish believed the other was encroaching on its space or because one parish believed the other to be driving evil spirits into its territory.

The village children would also participate and the procession would stop wherever there was a landmark such as a tree or big stone. There, one of the boys of the village would be beaten with willow branches. If there was a pond or stream beside the boundary, another boy would be ducked in the water. While it may now sound cruel, once you had taken part in 'beating the bounds', you remembered where the edge of your village was – and you didn't go beyond that boundary. Victims were usually rewarded with a silver coin. In Scotland, the custom is known as 'riding the marches' or 'common riding'.

Rogationtide was instituted as early as the year 511 when a

Church Council (the first Council of Orleans) ordered that the three days leading up to Ascension Day should be celebrated as Rogation Days. All work was cancelled so that everyone might join in the processions. In England, Rogationtide rituals, along with other processions, were suppressed by Protestants after the Reformation, but they were reinstated in the time of Queen Elizabeth I, being considered a proper way of seeking God's blessing. But in Tudor times and later, Rogationtide also remained a time for communal feasting and drinking, funded by local landowners. This not only created goodwill but also tended to reinforce the hierarchical structure of rural life. The poet and priest George Herbert, writing in the 1630s, expressed the very essence of the Rogation procession:

> There are contained therein four manifest advantages: first, a blessing of God for the fruits of the field; secondly, justice in the preservation of bounds; thirdly, charity in loving walking and neighbourly accompanying one another, with reconciling of differences at that time, if there be any; fourthly, mercy in relieving the poor by a liberal distribution and largesse ... wherefore he [the country parson] exacts of all to be present at the perambulation, and those that withdraw and sever themselves from it he mislikes, and reproves as uncharitable and unneighbourly.

Even today in some country villages, congregations perambulate around the fields nearest their church to ask a blessing on each field. In recent years, in places throughout Britain and the United States, there has been a renewed interest in Rogationtide as a time of celebration and prayer, a time set aside for recognition of our dependence on the land for our food and on God for the annual miracles of sprouting seeds, growing plants and maturing harvest. It has also become a time for thinking about our stewardship of the earth and environmental issues.

# *Ascension Day*

*The feast of the Ascension is one of the three great festivals of the Church's year, along with Christmas and Easter. It marks the end of Jesus' life on earth and his return to heaven.*

In Austria, in Belgium, Denmark and Finland, in France, Germany and the Netherlands, in Norway and Sweden, Ascension Day is a national holiday. In other countries (including Britain) people now take little notice of it and many in the secular world may be unaware of its existence. But, in times gone by, churches would be crowded at service time on this major festival. Today, even some church-goers seem uncomfortable with the concept of the Ascension, while in other churches, in order that it is not totally neglected, it is transferred to the next Sunday.

It comes at the end of 'the Forty Glorious Days', the period of rejoicing that follows Easter and counter-balances Lent. During those forty days, as the Gospel accounts tell us, Jesus appeared on several occasions to his followers. Then, as we read in the Acts of the Apostles, on the day we now call Ascension Day he led his closest friends to the top of a small hill just outside the city of Jerusalem. There, he repeated his promise made before the crucifixion that he would not leave them 'comfortless' but that the Holy Spirit would be with them always. Then (we are told), he was 'lifted up' and a low cloud covered the hilltop and hid him from them. When the

83

cloud lifted, he was gone. As heaven was commonly believed to be a place literally above the earth, there developed the belief that he had 'ascended'. To symbolize his physical departure from the earth, the Paschal candle (which is lit in many churches at Easter) is extinguished at Ascensiontide.

A senior clergyman once confessed that the story of the Ascension had always made him giggle: whenever he tried to imagine it, his mind filled with literal images as he began to picture some sort of invisible elevator. Perhaps it is the supernatural quality of the Ascension that makes some people uncomfortable with the celebration of an event which appears to defy the laws of science.

It is, of course, a glorious festival, a day of rejoicing that Christ's work has been completed, in triumph. In less scientific times, congregations had no trouble with its literal interpretation. In many churches, a statue of Jesus or a large crucifix would be lifted high above the altar. In a few places, it was hauled right up through a hole in the church roof and out of sight: a memorable and highly dramatic way of teaching the Ascension Day message.

The feast is one of great antiquity. Although no proof dating earlier than the fourth century exists, St Augustine spoke of it as originating in the time of the first apostles. That it is frequently mentioned by St John Chrysostom in the fourth century certainly suggests that it was then a well-established observance.

Important though it may be, few social customs have been connected with it, although it was probably a time for blessing the growing crops before the Rogation Days became a part of the calendar. Indeed, Ascension Day was the day on which many communities conducted the ceremony of beating the bounds (see p. 80) – including several distinctly 'non-rural' parishes within the City of London. Every three years, at the Tower of London, there is one such progress on Ascension Day around an area of land called the 'Tower Liberty'.

It dates from 1555 and is led by an official called the Chief Yeoman Warder. Following him come the Tower Officers, their wives and a gaoler carrying his axe. Local children also take part. When a boundary marker is now situated in the middle of a busy road, the Chief Yeoman Warder simply points to it, shouting 'Mark it well.' He is answered by a shout from the whole procession: 'Marked.'

There are other local customs associated with Ascension Day. In an area near Bangor in North Wales it used to be thought unlucky to work on that day. This was not due to religious observance but to a superstition that if work did take place, an accident in one of the nearby mines or quarries would occur. In Derbyshire, 'well-dressing' still happens at this time of year, one of the most famous ceremonies being at Tissington on Ascension Day itself. The custom survives from the days before piped water, and indeed from pre-Christian times. As a way of giving thanks for a natural supply of fresh water, people 'dressed' or decorated springs and wells. A board would be covered in clay and then an arrangement of flowers, moss, shells, twigs and fir cones would be pressed into the clay to make a bright and cheerful picture. Nothing artificial or machine-made was ever used in the collages and the clay was watered to keep the flowers fresh for several days.

In other places, well-dressing takes place on the next festival of the year: Pentecost.

# Pentecost

*The festival that commemorates the coming of the Holy Spirit (like 'tongues of fire') to the apostles in Jerusalem fifty days after the resurrection is now usually known in the ecclesiastical world as Pentecost. Until quite recently, it was better known throughout Britain as Whitsun.*

In present-day England, Whitsun is a word loosely applied to the late Spring Bank Holiday. As late as the middle of the twentieth century, however, it was a widely observed celebration that ranked close behind Christmas and Easter in importance. Especially in north-west England the whole week was a major secular holiday. Its highlight were the Whit Walks. At the head of these processions would march the local brass band. Then came children from various parishes (the girls always dressed in white) with their leaders carrying banners emblazoned with the name of their church or Sunday School. Following them marched parents, teachers and other adults.

In Manchester, the Anglican churches walked on Whit Monday. Led by the Bishop of Manchester and the cathedral choir, the procession wound its way through the shopping centre, whatever the weather. On Whit Friday, it was the turn of the Roman Catholics, led by the bishop of neighbouring Salford with Irish pipers happily playing both 'Land of Hope and Glory' and more conventional Irish tunes. In later years, the Italian community would parade a statue of the Virgin Mary.

The point of the processions, which grew out of the Victorian Sunday School movement, was to witness the faith. The name Whitsun comes from a much older name, White Sunday, for this was one of the festivals (the other being Easter) on which Christians were traditionally baptized. For this rite of passage they wore white clothes, hence the English name for the Sunday and subsequent week. A much earlier Whitsun tradition was the brewing of Whitsun-ale (or church-ale). This particularly strong brew was sold by the church to the local population to raise funds for church purposes.

In most countries (and now also in churches in Britain), the festival is more usually called Pentecost, this name deriving from the fact that it occurs fifty days after Easter, 'pente' in turn being derived from a Greek word for fifty. Although Whitsun used to be the more common English name, the word 'Pentecostal' was in use in past centuries. For example, 'Pentecostals' were offerings made at this time to the parish priest or curate. The word also applied to offerings made by a parish church to its diocesan cathedral.

Since Easter is a movable feast, so too is Pentecost. Consequently the English Whit Week holiday could occur any week from the second half of May to early June. In the late 1960s, legislation was passed to fix what is now officially called the Spring Bank Holiday on the last Monday of May. As a result, this holiday weekend does not always coincide with the Christian festival and consequently the secular world is now often scarcely aware of Pentecost.

But for Christians it is a reminder of the occasion, fifty days after the resurrection of Jesus, when his disciples met to pray in an upstairs room in Jerusalem – possibly the same room in which they had shared a last supper with him the night before his crucifixion. As they were praying (so we read in the second chapter of the New Testament book The Acts of the Apostles), there suddenly came a sound like 'the rush of a mighty wind'. They saw what appeared to be tongues of fire on each of their heads but they were not harmed in any way. From this sign, they deduced that this was the realization of Christ's promise that he would send them (and all Christians) his Holy Spirit as a source of strength and comfort. Since the apostles immediately went into the streets to preach the faith and to seek converts for the first time, Pentecost is sometimes called the birthday of the Church.

The first Christian Pentecost is also commemorated in the mitre (or flame-shaped head-dress) worn on ceremonial occasions by bishops, the successors of the original apostles. Different localities have their own specific traditions. In Italy, it used to be the custom to scatter red rose petals from the ceilings of churches to recall the tongues of fire and there the feast is known as *Pascha rossa* because the vestments worn at this time are coloured red for the same reason. At a village called El Rocio in Spain a statue of Mary, the mother of Jesus, and the infant Jesus is carried in a huge procession. In some French churches, trumpets are sounded as a reminder of the rushing wind, while in other communities the festival is marked by the release of a white dove, the traditional symbol in art for the Holy Spirit because the third chapter of Matthew's Gospel tells us that, at his baptism, the Holy Spirit descended on Jesus 'like a dove'. Until the Reformation, a number of doves were released inside St Paul's Cathedral in London as great clouds of incense billowed around them. Another continental custom that has occasionally been copied has been the flying of kites to illustrate the all-pervading presence of the Holy Spirit. More than one minister who has attempted to borrow this custom has been defeated by a dead calm.

One reason Jesus' disciples had assembled in the upper room may have been to mark the Jewish festival of Shavuot or Spring Harvest (also known as Pentecost because it occurs fifty days after Passover) which celebrates the first fruits of the fields, especially the early wheat. For this reason the foods associated with the festival include specially baked loaves made in the shape of sheaves of corn; and also dairy products, notably these days cheesecake. During Shavuot, many synagogues look as if they are holding flower festivals as they are decorated with sheaves of corn or barley, lilies and other flowers – but Shavuot also commemorates the Giving of the Law by God to Moses on Mount Sinai and its acceptance by the Jewish people. For this reason, Pentecost can be said to mark the founding of both the Jewish and Christian religions. (See also Lammas, p. 99.)

# Trinity

*Trinity Sunday, the festival honouring the threefold nature of God (Father, Son and Holy Spirit) is a comparatively recent addition to the Christian year. It is observed on the Sunday following Pentecost because, with the coming of the Holy Spirit to the first apostles on that day, all three manifestations of God have been completed.*

Despite the sometimes difficult or even abstract nature of the doctrine of the Trinity ('One in Three, Three in One'), the origins of this festival were very much at the grass roots of the Church. From around the year 800, it was a genuinely popular celebration in several parts of northern Europe – especially in Germany, France and England. In Ireland, the three-leafed shamrock became a national emblem because, it was said, St Patrick (who first preached Christianity there) used the plant to teach the doctrine of the Trinity.

The observance of Trinity Sunday did not, however, at first meet with official approval. By the eleventh century, its celebration was being discouraged by the Pope, Alexander II, on the grounds that a festival in honour of the Trinity was unnecessary since the Trinity was regularly honoured in the saying of the *Gloria Patri* ('Glory be to the Father and to the Son and to the Holy Ghost . . .').

That seems to have done little to diminish its observance and it gained a special prominence in England following the martyrdom of Thomas Becket, Archbishop of Canterbury, in his own cathedral in the year 1170. He had been made archbishop on or very near Trinity Sunday in the year 1162, and following his death the festival's popularity was greatly boosted. This was reflected in the Sarum Rite, the form of service used in Salisbury Cathedral, which was given its definitive form by Richard Poore who was Bishop of Salisbury from 1220 to 1228. In the Sarum Rite (which was adopted by several other English cathedrals), the Sundays in the second half of the year were numbered after Trinity rather than after Pentecost, as was (and still is) the custom of the Roman Catholic Church.

Eventually, in 1334, Pope John XXII ordered the recognition of Trinity Sunday as a festival day by the whole of the western Church and it has since become a day appointed for ordinations to the priesthood. It also marks the end of the first half of the Church's year. From Advent to Trinity, the calendar (and indeed the appointed Gospel readings) can be said to focus on what Jesus did; from Trinity onwards, the emphasis is on what he taught.

When Thomas Cranmer edited the first Book of Common Prayer in 1549, he preserved the Sarum usage of numbering the Sundays of the second half of the year as 'Sundays after Trinity', a custom that was maintained until 1980 when the new Anglican *Alternative Service Book* fell into line with the Roman Catholic Church in numbering the Sundays after Pentecost. Twenty years later, when the Anglican Church replaced that book with *Common Worship*, it reverted to its former tradition of numbering the Sundays 'after Trinity'.

These Sundays (from the First Sunday after Trinity until the Sunday next before Advent) and also the variable number of Sundays that fall between the Presentation of Christ (or Candlemas) and the start of Lent are termed 'Ordinary Time'. The word 'ordinary' is not used in this context as meaning common or mundane but derives from the word 'ordinal', which means 'defining position'. (The ordinal numbers are the words 'first', 'second', 'third', etc. – as opposed to the cardinal numbers 'one', 'two', 'three', etc.) The opposite of Ordinary Time is Sacred Time, which comprises the seasons before and after Christmas and the part of the year that lasts from Ash Wednesday, through Lent and Eastertide, until Trinity Sunday.

Trinity Sunday is not observed by the eastern Churches which keep this day as the Festival of the Holy Martyrs.

# Corpus Christi

*Corpus Christi is the last of the big festivals of the Church's year in the sequence which leads from Advent through Christmas to Easter, the Ascension and Pentecost. Like Pentecost, Corpus Christi (which follows ten days later) is a reminder that, although Jesus returned to his Father in heaven, God still lives on earth.*

In Northern Ireland, summer is the marching season. Protestant groups parade through the streets to demonstrate their loyalties. In different parts of Britain, other parades and processions take place in high summer. Luton has its multicultural carnival; the Notting Hill district of London holds its celebration in August. During the last century, similar events were often organized by trade unions – the most famous being the Durham Miners' Gala. For over two centuries, some of the most popular and widespread processions were those held on the day known as Corpus Christi, a Latin name meaning 'the body of Christ'.

Corpus Christi was (and is) a movable feast since it is observed in Europe on the Thursday ten days after Pentecost, which in turn occurs fifty days after Easter. In the United States and a few other countries it is observed on the Sunday two weeks after Pentecost. Its origins date from the year 1208. In that year, a Belgian nun called Juliana had a vision of a dazzling bright disc, a little like the moon – but it was marred by one dark spot. She came to believe her vision was a message from God telling her that the disc was imperfect because the church calendar had no special feast day to honour the sacrament of the Eucharist. Her vision caught the imagination of the people of her time and in 1264 the festival was given official approval by the Pope, Urban IV. Of course, many Christians feel that the proper time to give thanks for Holy Communion is on the evening of Maundy Thursday at a commemoration of the Last Supper, but there are those who think that because Maundy Thursday is in Lent and so close to Good Friday, that is not an apt time of year for a cheerful thanksgiving. So the feast or festival of Corpus Christi, celebrated on a Thursday in early June, came to be universally observed by the western Church during the mid-fourteenth century.

In England, it was first observed in the year 1318 and quickly established itself as a major and a popular holiday, its popularity being testified by the various guilds and colleges named in its honour. It was marked by processions in which the holy sacrament was paraded with all due ceremony through the streets of the town – one of only two occasions in the year (the other being Palm Sunday) on which the sacrament was normally taken outside a church. For the medieval man or woman, simply to see or to be in the presence of the sacrament was both an honour and a blessing.

Soon after its establishment in England, Corpus Christi acquired a drama festival. At this time, the trade unions (or guilds as they were then called) began staging what came to be known as Mystery Plays – so called because they taught the largely illiterate people the mysteries of Christianity. They were acted on wooden stages or wagons which were trundled through the streets of cities that included Chester, Coventry, Wakefield and York. If you stood in one place, the procession of plays (in biblical order) would trundle past you from dawn to dusk.

The long daylight hours of Corpus Christi made it an

especially suitable day for the performance of these plays. Each play was rehearsed and acted by members of an appropriate guild. So, at Chester, the watermen (not boatmen but men who delivered supplies of water around the city) acted the story of Noah and the Flood. In York, the nail-makers performed the story of the crucifixion while the bakers acted the story especially connected with the festival of Corpus Christi: the Last Supper. A pageant master settled disputes and ensured the wagons (and plays) arrived at each performance point in the right order.

Many of the plays acquired comic scenes that were decidedly non-biblical. For example, at Wakefield in Yorkshire, the play about the first Christmas Eve (telling how the shepherds on the hillside near Bethlehem visited the infant Jesus) had as its principal plot a story about a distinctly northern shepherd called Mak who tries to steal a young sheep belonging to one of the other shepherds. He takes it home and, when the other shepherds come looking for it, hides it in a cradle and pretends his wife has just had a baby – until the sheep starts bleating.

'Let me lift up the cloth and give your baby a kiss,' says one of the shepherds.

Mak fails to stop him, his theft is uncovered and, as a punishment, he is tossed up and down in a blanket. Then, with a sudden change of gear, an angel tells the shepherds of the birth of the Christ Child and they take gifts to the stable, falling down there in worship. We are unsure which guild performed this play at Wakefield but a similar one at Coventry was acted by the sheep-shearers and tailors.

Following the Reformation, observance of Corpus Christi declined (in some cases quite abruptly) in the mainly Protestant countries of northern Europe. In England, the 1559 Act of Uniformity abolishing the mass and reintroducing the English prayer book became law on 24 June that year – outlawing such observances. Even so, at Canterbury that summer, a crowd of over 3,000 joined in the Corpus Christi procession in a demonstration of allegiance to the traditional ceremonies.

The day remained an important festival in the Roman Catholic Church and processions and celebrations still take place in Catholic countries. In Spain and many South and Central American countries there are colourful street processions which still include examples of street drama as well as music and dancing. Statues of the saints are paraded through the streets. In Cuzco in Peru, a statue of the patron saint of each church (freshly painted and dressed in new robes) is carried in a colourful procession to the local cathedral. There the statues remain for a week before being returned to their own churches. In Seville in Spain, the sacrament itself is carried through streets packed with cheering crowds and echoing with the sound of every church bell in the city. In Italy, a festival called *Corpus Domini* (meaning 'the body of the Lord') is held one Sunday in June. At Genzano di Roma (a town near Rome) there is a famous *Infiorata* or flower festival when a huge carpet of flowers is created in the town.

In recent years, the observance of Corpus Christi has been revived in Anglican parishes (and not only in 'high church' ones). It is included in the calendar of the present Church of England prayer book, *Common Worship*, as 'the Day of Thanksgiving for the Institution of Holy Communion'.

# Lammas

*Long before Christian harvest festivals were held to commemorate the completion of the harvest, it was usual to celebrate the start of the corn harvest. On 1 August, it became the custom to bring to church a loaf made from the first corn to be harvested and for that loaf to be consecrated in thanksgiving for the new harvest.*

Pagans in Britain, as in many European countries, celebrated the feast of one of their favourite gods, the sun god Lugh, at the beginning of August. His actual feast day was the first day of the month, although the celebrations encompassed both the preceding and the following fortnights – but the feast was also partly a wake in that it marked the fading of the sun god's power as winter approached. Known as Lughnasadh, the festival survived the coming of Christianity as a Gaelic holiday celebrated on 1 August. Some Irish people continue to celebrate it with bonfires and dancing. The word *Lughnasadh* remains the modern Gaelic term for the month of August.

Elsewhere, as Christianity spread northwards through the continent, Christians began to take over this and similar pagan festivals and simultaneously to develop a Christian version of the Jewish Festival of First Fruits, often called Shavuot (see Pentecost, pp. 87–90). Indeed, in the *Anglo-Saxon Chronicle* (the chronological record of events compiled by monks in the Middle Ages), there are frequent references to 'the feast of first fruits' and the duty of tenants to present newly harvested wheat to their landlords on 1 August.

The feast of first fruits eventually evolved into Lammas, the word being derived from the Old English word *hlaf*, meaning 'loaf' ('mass' meaning festival) – and absorbed some of the customs associated with Lughnasadh. At Lammas time, the first sheaf of wheat was ceremonially reaped, threshed, milled and baked into a loaf and then used in the sacrament of Holy Communion – the grain dying so that the people might have 'the bread of life'. Even so, Lammas (like its pagan precursor) was a day for both rejoicing and anxiety: pleasure that the crops were ripening, anxiety that a storm might yet spoil the harvest. It is only in comparatively recent times that Lammas has declined in importance but it is still observed in a number of West Country churches with the 'first loaf' being used as the bread at Holy Communion services.

Lammastide became a popular time for country fairs where farmers could sell their produce and people could buy what they needed for the winter months. It was also a time for sporting competitions and music-making. Lammas fairs survive in some places, such as Ballycastle in County Antrim in Northern Ireland, while the city of Exeter maintains a tradition dating back to pre-Norman times.

In Scotland, Lammas is (like Lady Day) one of the legal 'quarter days' of the year. Coincidentally, the date was formerly observed by the Roman Catholic Church as the feast day of 'St Peter in Chains', a day which commemorated his release from prison as described in the book of the Acts of the Apostles.

# Harvest

*Unlike the United States and Canada, there is no set date in Britain for this celebration but harvest festivals are usually held in either the second half of September or the first week of October.*

Morwenstow is a village on the north coast of Cornwall. In 1843, its vicar was the Reverend Robert Stephen Hawker who was, incidentally, also a poet and enthusiastic opium user. That September, he announced, 'God has been very merciful to us this year. He hath filled our garners with increase, and satisfied our poor with bread . . . Let us offer a sacrifice of thanksgiving.' Thus was initiated what we now think of as the traditional English harvest festival. Victorian hymns such as 'We plough the fields and scatter', 'Come, ye thankful people, come' and 'All things bright and beautiful' helped popularize his idea of harvest thanksgiving, and the custom of decorating churches with local produce became widespread.

Parishioners often spend a great deal of time decorating their church. Apples are arranged along window sills, bunches of grapes are hung from unlikely places and vegetables are arranged along steps, while bunches of wheat or barley are made to stand by the choir stalls. There are often displays of specially made loaves, trays of eggs and bunches of flowers – even, these days, tinned food. Each gift represents a 'thank you' for food that has grown during the summer and which will keep the population fed during the coming winter. In some seaside churches, fishermen bring some of their catch to be part of the thanksgiving. In others, coal miners used to offer the coal they had dug from deep in the earth: Harvest is, after all, a thanksgiving for all the 'fruits' of the earth. When the festival is over, the food is either given away to those in need or sold and the money given to the poor in this or other countries. Any flowers are sent to local hospitals.

Harvest-time is actually one of the world's oldest festivals and was celebrated by the Ancient Greeks, who gave thanks to Demeter the goddess of agriculture, and by the Romans, who called her Ceres. The Jewish people have celebrated harvest or Sukkot (the Feast of the Tabernacles) for over 3,000 years. The name Sukkot refers to the huts (*sukkah*) that Moses and the Israelites lived in while wandering in the desert before reaching the Promised Land. These huts were made of branches and were easy to assemble, to take apart, and to carry as the Israelites wandered through the desert. Many Jewish families still build a *sukkah* at harvest time and decorate it with apples, grapes, corn, pomegranates and other fruit and vegetables.

Although the Christian harvest festival may be comparatively modern in origin, the celebration of the harvest in Britain pre-dates Christianity. As we have seen, farmers would offer the first cut sheaf of corn to one of their fertility gods, in the hope of receiving a good harvest – a tradition which developed into Lammas. Meanwhile the last sheaf to be cut (at the end of the harvest) was thought to contain the Spirit of the Corn, and its cutting was usually accompanied by the ritual sacrifice of an animal – sometimes a hare caught hiding in the corn. Later, the sacrificial animal was replaced by a model hare made from straw – a custom that led to the plaiting of 'corn dollies' which were hung in farmhouses until the following year. The horse bringing home the last cartload of corn was decorated with garlands of flowers and colourful ribbons.

In the days when farming was a largely unmechanized industry, harvesting was a long and tiring job – and often a battle against the weather. Consequently, its completion was an occasion for much feasting. When the harvest was 'safely gathered in', a celebratory supper was held to which the whole community was invited. For many of the farm workers, this meal, known as the 'harvest-home', was the biggest and best meal of the year – until Christmas, at least. The custom survives in the harvest suppers still held in many rural communities.

# All Hallows

*The Christian holy days of All Saints and All Souls were imposed upon the pagan festival of Samhain. Of late, the commercial and secular worlds have, to a certain extent, reinvented that earlier celebration of the powers of darkness.*

In recent years the American Hallowe'en custom of 'trick or treat' has become commonplace in Britain as well as in other countries. On the evening of 31 October, children go from house to house, knocking on the front door and asking 'Trick or treat?' The householder then has the supposed choice of offering their young visitors a treat in the form of something sweet to eat or money – or saying no. In the latter case, the children feel they have a licence to play a trick. Traditional ones have included emptying a dustbin in the pathway or rubbing soap on a window.

It is a custom that has its dangers. There have been cases of trick-or-treaters being given drugs instead of sweets or of being persuaded to enter strangers' houses. On the other hand, many elderly people feel threatened by their night-time visitors and have been bullied into parting with by-no-means small amounts of money. The tricks in some cases have escalated to include breaking windows. Even so, it remains a popular activity, often encouraged by parents.

Hallowe'en has also, in recent years, become a commercial festival, rated by some as being second only to Christmas.

Shops and supermarkets are full of 'spooky' fancy dress costumes and masks – many relating to witches who have long been said to be particularly active on this night. Pumpkins have suddenly become widely available in stores – not so much to be eaten as to be hollowed out to make lanterns. Turnips are also used for this purpose. After being hollowed out, slits are cut in the shape of eyes, nose and mouth and a candle is placed inside to make a ghostly, grinning face.

The celebration of Hallowe'en predates the Christian era. The peoples of northern Europe believed that, as the winter nights got longer and darkness prevailed, evil spirits became stronger. In the Celtic countries, especially in Scotland and Ireland, a day approximately halfway between the autumn equinox and the winter solstice (31 October) was celebrated as Samhain, which literally means 'summer's end'. So Samhain marked the first day of winter when cattle and sheep were led down from their hillside pastures to winter in stables and byres – just as Beltane (see May Day, pp. 73–5) marked the beginning of the season.

At Samhain, sacrifices were offered up in thanksgiving for the harvest and bonfires were lit – a custom that survived until the First World War. Young people would light brands from the fires and run around the fields and farms. Afterwards, ashes from the fires were sprinkled over the fields to protect them during the winter months – a custom which, of course, improved the soil. These bonfire festivals provided islands of light within the oncoming tide of winter darkness, a seasonal custom that has been transferred to 5 November to commemorate Guy Fawkes' failure in 1605 to blow up Parliament.

The ancient Celts also saw Samhain as a spiritual time, a potent time for communion with departed spirits. The 'veil between the worlds' of the living and the dead was said to be at its thinnest on this day so the dead were invited to return to feast with their loved ones, welcomed in from the cold.

Ancient customs ranged from leaving food out for dead ancestors to the performance of rituals to encourage communication with those who had passed over. These rituals were thought to be best presided over by witches and sorcerers, so Samhain also became associated with witches, black cats (the 'familiars' or animal friends of witches), bats (because of their nocturnal habits) and all manner of ghosts. The stereotypical witch riding a broomstick is derived from more recent fairy tales, but what is now thought to be a harmless Hallowe'en game of apple bobbing, in which you have to see how many apples you can retrieve from a large bowl of water using only your mouth, has its antecedents in a traditional method of telling fortunes.

Parallel with the continuing observance of Samhain and similar observances in other northern countries was the development of the Christian festival of All Saints. The first All Saints' Day occurred on 13 May 609, when Pope Boniface IV accepted the Pantheon building in Rome as a gift from the emperor. Boniface dedicated it as a church and named the church and day in honour of the Virgin Mary and All Martyrs. During Pope Gregory III's reign (731–41), the festival was expanded to include all saints who have no saint's day of their own, and a chapel in St Peter's church was dedicated accordingly. The feast day was officially designated All Saints' Day in 837 by Pope Gregory IV, and although this festival has since been observed by eastern churches on the first Sunday after Pentecost, it is observed by the western churches on 1 November as All Saints' or All Hallows' Day (to hallow meaning to make holy). In this way the Church was able to harness and counteract the pagan Samhain customs of the night before – an evening that gradually became known as All Hallows' Eve or Hallowe'en.

All Saints was an important holiday in Britain until the Reformation resulted in less honour being given to the saints, but it remains a holiday in Austria, Belgium, France,

Germany, Italy and Spain. It is interesting to speculate whether it is the down-playing of All Saints as a holiday that has created a vacuum in which Hallowe'en has reasserted itself as a means of providing 'cheer' during the darkness of late autumn and early winter.

All Saints' Day is followed by All Souls' Day, also known as 'the day of the dead' or Deads' Day. This is a time not just for remembering saints or holy people who have died but as a remembrance of everyone who has died. In some countries (especially those of Central America) families visit cemeteries to put flowers on the graves of their loved ones. Although some may dismiss it as a cult of the dead, it is a chance to remember shared happy times and to pray or give thanks that the souls of loved ones may now be at peace and enjoying the promise of heaven.

All Souls' Day absorbed the primitive belief that this was a season when the dead returned to earth to taste ordinary food again, so there was (in some places in Britain) a custom of placing a glass of wine and cakes (known as soul cakes) on family graves. Over the years, the custom changed and people would go 'a-souling'. That is, in groups they would visit the larger houses in the area, singing a song which asked for soul cakes:

> Soul, soul, for a soul cake!
> I pray, good mistress, for a soul cake!

Again, it is interesting to speculate whether it was a folk memory of this activity that led to trick or treating.

# *Martinmas and Remembrance Day*

*In the United Kingdom, Remembrance Sunday is the second Sunday in November and is now a time to remember and honour all those who have died in wars since and including the First World War. Originally the dead of that war were remembered on the exact anniversary of Armistice Day: 11 November. For centuries before this date became Armistice Day, it was a feast day in honour of St Martin, a former Roman soldier.*

For the Anglo-Saxons, this was the time of year for killing: killing the pigs, sheep and cattle it would be too expensive to feed and house during the cold winter months. The best meat was salted or pickled to preserve it. Sides of beef and bacon were hung in chimneys and smoked over a fire so they too would keep longer. That left the question of what to do with the rest of the meat, the offal. The solution was to have a feast, especially as the new season's beer was ready for drinking. Popular seasonal sports included pig-baiting, cock-fighting and wrestling. But as Christianity took hold in northern Europe, this pagan festival (like so many others) was 'Christianized' – and became Martinmas, the saint's day of St Martin.

Martin was born around the year 316, was brought up in Italy and at the age of 15 joined the Roman army. At 18, he was made an officer and posted to Amiens in France. One winter's evening, it is said, he was riding on horseback through the town, with his soldiers marching behind him. Meeting a half-naked beggar, Martin stopped and, with one swift movement, cut his red officer's cloak in two and gave one half to the beggar. That night, Martin dreamed he saw Jesus wearing half his cloak. He was baptized, refused to continue fighting and was imprisoned, but was eventually discharged from the army. In 371, he became Bishop of Tours. One of the many traditions associated with Martin states that he was crushed by a mill wheel. Accordingly, in Ireland and the Scottish Western Isles, it became the custom that 'No woman should spin on that day; no miller should grind his corn, and no wheel should be turned.'

Completely coincidentally, it was on his feast day that the First World War came to an end. At five o'clock that morning, the Armistice was signed in a railway carriage in northern France and six hours later, at the eleventh hour of the eleventh day of the eleventh month, the guns fell silent. In a letter published in the London *Evening News* on 8 May 1919, an Australian journalist, Edward George Honey, proposed 'a respectful silence' to remember those who had given their lives. This came to the attention of King George V and, on 7 November, he issued a proclamation calling for a two-minute silence so that 'the thoughts of everyone may be concentrated on reverent remembrance of the glorious dead'. That first two-minute silence was reported in the *Manchester Guardian* the following morning:

The first stroke of eleven produced a magical effect. The tramcars glided into stillness, motors ceased to cough and fume, and stopped dead, and the mighty-limbed dray horses hunched back on their loads and stopped also, seeming to do it of their own volition. Someone took off his hat, and with a nervous hesitancy the rest of the men bowed their heads also. Here and there an old soldier could be detected slipping unconsciously into the posture of 'attention'.

It was only after the end of the Second World War in 1945 that what had previously been known as Armistice Day became Remembrance Day, to include those who had fallen in both wars (and now in subsequent wars). From 1955, Remembrance Day was observed on the second Sunday of November rather than on the eleventh day of the month but since the fiftieth anniversary (in 1995) of the ending of the Second World War, it has become usual to observe both Armistice Day and Remembrance Sunday.

Each Remembrance Day is marked by ceremonies at local war memorials and in many churches, often attended by civic dignitaries, men and women who formerly served in the fighting forces; and sometimes members of youth organizations such as the Scouts, Guides and cadet forces. Wreaths of poppies are laid on memorials and the two-minute silence is observed. The nation's principal ceremony is held at the Cenotaph in Whitehall in London and is attended by the monarch, the prime minister, leaders of the political parties and representatives of the Commonwealth.

The Cenotaph itself was originally constructed out of wood and plaster as a temporary focus for the Victory Parade following the First World War, held on 19 July 1919. There was widespread approval of the hastily prepared design by Edwin Lutyens and the government commissioned a re-creation of the design as the permanent national war memorial. It was unveiled on 11 November 1920 and the first Ceremony of Remembrance took place the following year.

The poppy became the symbol of remembrance because so many grew on what had once been the battlefields of the First World War.

Remembrance Sunday is not marked in every church: there are some who feel that it runs the risk of glorifying war. Its true purpose remains, however, to honour those who lost their lives while fighting for freedom and justice; and to support those who survived but suffered.

In the United States of America, Armistice Day was renamed Veterans' Day in 1954. Government legislation tried in 1971 to move it to the fourth Monday in October to create a three-day weekend. The move proved unpopular and since 1978 it has been marked on 11 November – as it always has been in Canada.

# *Thanksgiving*

*The first North American Thanksgivings were harvest festivals and pre-date the English harvest festival as we now know it. Latterly, Thanksgiving has become a family celebration (often rivalling or equalling Christmas in significance) but for many it remains a religious event.*

The very first American Thanksgiving was offered by a small band of English settlers when they reached what is now Virginia, where they marked their safe arrival with prayer but no feast. Then, in 1620, a larger number of English settlers who had crossed the Atlantic on the sailing ship *Mayflower* landed at Plymouth, in New England. A harsh winter took the lives of many, but by the summer of 1621 a good harvest was in prospect and the Pilgrims (as they were named) held a three-day-long celebration, feeding on turkeys, geese, ducks and deer. Other settlements in the area (now known by its American Indian name of Massachusetts) began to copy this concept of harvest thanksgivings. There was, however, no set date – a situation which still prevails in Britain.

Over the years, it developed into a thanksgiving for more than the harvest. During the American War of Independence (1775–83), General George Washington decreed eight days were to be considered days of thanksgiving for victories over the British 'rendering under Almighty God our sincere and humble thanks'. In 1789, by when he had become the first president, he named 26 November as a day of national thanksgiving. In the same year, leaders of the American churches ordained the first Thursday in November as a day for thanksgiving. Despite these rulings, different states continued to hold thanksgiving celebrations on varying dates until, in 1863, President Abraham Lincoln ordered that the last Thursday in November should be a national day of thanksgiving.

In 1939, apparently in order to boost the pre-Christmas shopping season, President Franklin D. Roosevelt brought the festival one week forward. Not every state fell into line, and two years later Congress reinstated the fourth Thursday of November as Thanksgiving, making it a national public holiday. During the twentieth century, it was increasingly marked by parades which include not only many participants in fancy dress but numbers of inflatable balloons in the shape of modern cartoon characters, high school bands and even Santa Claus. It also became a day for games of American football, though these are now likely to be played on the Saturday of what has become a holiday weekend.

Special services are held on the morning of Thanksgiving Day – not only in churches but also in synagogues and other places of worship. The main event of the day, however, is the family meal, which many may not regard as a harvest meal but which nevertheless traditionally contains many reminders of the early harvest thanksgivings: turkey, sweet potato, cranberry sauce and pumpkin pie.

Although the original Pilgrim Fathers were deeply religious and although Thanksgiving does retain a religious element, it now also reflects the multi-faith and secular aspects of American society. For this reason, and because, unlike Christmas, it can be celebrated by followers of all faiths and of none, Thanksgiving is likely to increase its pre-eminence in the calendar of American festivals.

In Canada, Thanksgiving is also a family holiday but, reflecting that country's earlier harvests, it is observed in October – since 1957 on the second Monday in October.

# *Index*